# Faith and History in the Old Testament

# Faith and History
# in the
# Old Testament

R. A. F. MacKenzie, s.j.

THE MACMILLAN COMPANY
*New York*

COLLIER-MACMILLAN LIMITED
*London*

*Imprimi potest:*
Gordon George, S.J.
*Praep. prov.*


*Imprimatur:*
✠ Francis V. Allen
*die 23 ianuarii 1963*


The statements above have no reference to the role of the University Press in publishing this book, since as a department of the University of Minnesota the Press naturally respects the separation of church and state.

Original edition published by the University of Minnesota Press, Minneapolis, Minnesota. Hard cover edition available from the University of Minnesota Press.

The Macmillan Company, New York
Collier-Macmillan Canada Ltd., Toronto, Ontario


Library of Congress Catalog Card Number: 63-10585

Printed in the United States of America

Third Printing 1968

# Foreword

FOR THE PAST several years, the University of Minnesota has been the beneficiary of a generous financial grant from the Danforth Foundation. The purpose of this grant, which is entirely separate from the regular program of Danforth lecturers supported by the same foundation, was to make it possible for the university to bring to its campus a number of distinguished scholars, representing major religious traditions, who would teach and lecture in the area of theology. The scholars who have participated have held the position of visiting professor and have offered a series of public lectures and a seminar open to advanced undergraduates and graduate students. The entire program has been under the direct supervision of the university's Department of Philosophy with the advice and cooperation of the university coordinator of student religious activities, Professor Henry Allen, and members of the Council of Religious Advisors, as well as many other members of the university faculty and administration.

The first scholar appointed to a visiting professorship under this program was Professor R. A. F. MacKenzie, S.J., of the Jesuit Seminary in Toronto (now Regis College). The present volume is based on the series of public lectures he gave during the winter quarter of 1960, on "The Theological Significance of the Old Testament." These lectures represented "an attempt to show the remarkable relevance of Israel's thought and experience to some of our modern religious problems." They were enthusiastically received by the university community and the public in general and the University Press is fortunate in being able to make them available to a still wider audience.

On behalf of the university, I wish to take this opportunity to thank Professor MacKenzie once again for the contribution he made while he was with us. Apart from his

5

regular responsibilities, his seminar and public lectures, he rendered many valuable extracurricular services, from appearances before numerous groups both on and off the university campus to countless informal discussions with other faculty members. We are also grateful, of course, to the Danforth Foundation and to his superiors at the Jesuit Seminary in Toronto, who jointly made his visit to the University of Minnesota possible.

Other visiting professors under the program of theological lectureships, in keeping with the intent of the donor that a wide variety of religious points of view should be represented, have been Professor Abraham Joshua Heschel, of the Jewish Theological Seminary of America, Bishop Anders Nygren, retired Lutheran Bishop of Lund, Sweden, Professor Emeritus William F. Albright, of the Johns Hopkins University, and Professor Emeritus Brand Blanshard of Yale University. Professor Julian Hartt gave a special series of Summer Session lectures. In addition to the present volume, there will be published volumes based on various of the series of lectures mentioned above—one or more by the University of Minnesota Press and others, because of prior commitments on the part of lecturers, by the Muhlenberg Press and the Free Press, a division of the Macmillan Company.

D. BURNHAM TERRELL
Chairman, Department of Philosophy

*February 1963*

# Preface

THE EIGHT LECTURES contained in this book were delivered at the University of Minnesota during the winter quarter, January to March 1960. They were presented before a general audience and hence were intended to be nontechnical in style, while sufficiently informative to appeal to men and women seriously interested in the background of Judaism and Christianity. They are printed here practically as they were given, with some minor omissions and corrections.

I am acutely aware how little in them is original, and how much I am indebted for my ideas to a host of books, some of them read many years ago. In most cases it is not possible for me now to sort out and ascribe to their original sources insights whose origins I have long since forgotten. If some scholar recognizes his pet discovery here repeated without acknowledgment, I must plead guilty and hope to cover myself to some degree by the inclusion of a selected bibliography. This brief list contains not necessarily the latest books on the subject, but those from which I have learned most in the past. The authors of course are not to be held responsible for the oversimplification or one-sidedness of some of my outlines, a result of the attempt to cover such a vast material in a limited time.

For permission to reprint copyright material, I am deeply indebted to Professor George E. Mendenhall, of the University of Michigan, and Professor David N. Freedman, of Pittsburgh Seminary. The translations from original texts are my own.

It is a pleasure to recall and to acknowledge here the kindness and generous hospitality shown to me by many persons during my stay in the Twin Cities. In particular, I wish to record my thanks to the following: to the Danforth Foundation, which made posible my engagement by the University; to Professor E. W. McDiarmid, dean of the

College of Science, Literature, and the Arts; to the then chairman of the Department of Philosophy, Dr. Alan Donagan, and his wife, for their cordial hospitality; to the other members of the department at that time, in particular Dr. Paul Holmer; to Professor Henry E. Allen, coordinator of Students' Religious Activities; to the Reverend George Garrelts and the staff of the Newman Center, who received me so kindly as a guest; finally, to the director of the University of Minnesota Press, John Ervin, Jr., for his helpfulness and above all for his patience.

R. A. F. M.

*Regis College*
*February 1963*

# Contents

# Faith and History in the Old Testament

Chapter 1

# The Quest for Salvation

IT MAY NOT be out of place to begin with a word in defense of the claim of theology to a hearing, among all the manifold intellectual activities that are represented on a university campus. In the College of Science, Literature, and the Arts, is there a place for theology, and what should that place be? Is theology to be ranked with music and dance and sculpture among the arts? Or is it, as a body of written material, part of literature? The answer is, it belongs properly to neither. Confidently the theologian will affirm that his specialty finds a place among the sciences.

This claim may sound presumptuous, to some even absurd; but let us remember that science is distinguished from art, for example, by its method, not by the material it works on. Theology has claimed and claims that its method is the properly scientific one of observation, collection, and classification of data, the hypothetic enunciation of laws which may explain those data, the experimental verification of such laws where possible, and the establishment with more or less certitude of factual conclusions. Granted, the data are of a very different kind from what the physical scientist is accustomed to working with. They include material from the humanities, the social sciences, history, and practically every other science that deals with man. But above and beyond that, this science derives its material from a source that is called "revelation."

Here of course we come to that which sets theology apart. Theology presupposes that an infinite and transcendent Being has communicated to man something of his own superior knowledge, has manifested himself to man in a way that is, at least in part, intellectually comprehensible. The scientific exercise of theology claims to be the application of human reason and understanding, of scientific

method and historical investigation, to this datum or starting point, which itself is not open to question.

I have no desire to disguise or evade the truth, that theology does not validate the datum on which it works. Just
as the physical scientist must take for granted the validity
of sense perception, the significant value of change and
process, the techniques of mathematics with which he cal-
culates, the principles of logic with which he reasons, so
the raw material of theology is, quite literally, something
taken on faith.

Now it is open to anyone to object that this makes it
only a pseudo-science; and the theologian as such cannot
refute that objection. By pseudo-science we understand a
corpus of doctrines and conclusions, logically and consistently worked out, whose datum or point of departure is
considered false and unacceptable. There have been such
pseudo-sciences. We need only think of astrology, which
rested on the principle that the movements of the heavenly
bodies had some—perhaps a decisive—influence on the
fortunes and destinies of men. Astrology erected a vast
structure of doctrine, reasonings, and pragmatic skills. But
they all remain bombinations in a vacuum for people who
do not accept the principle on which astrology is based.
Similarly with alchemy, the medieval pursuit of transmu-
tation of substances. Or, to come nearer to our own
subject, Mohammedan theology is a brilliant technical
construction of human thought, but its datum is the validity of the Koran as a text containing unchallengeable com-
munications of superhuman knowledge dictated to the
Prophet by an angelic messenger. Mohammedan theology
will be defective to one who finds the revelation to be a
mixture of truth and falsehood. It may seem a sheer waste
of time to one who entirely disbelieves in the genuineness
of any so-called revelation.

Therefore we must recognize the fact that any theology
rests ultimately on a basis of personal commitment. Its
*raison d' être* is an act of faith made by the theologian in
the validity of the datum which he proceeds to discuss and
analyze. His activity then is what Anselm called it: *fides*

*quaerens intellectum*, faith seeking to understand better that which it believes.

But can this activity be of any interest to others who do not share or do not fully share the theologian's fundamental commitment? I certainly believe it can. First, because if it represents an ancient and widespread religious tradition he will be presenting a doctrine which has governed the lives of millions of people, and has therefore a claim on the interest of any student of the humanities and of human experience. The Christian humanist, for example, should surely be sympathetically interested in an exposition of Mohammedan faith and doctrine. But, secondly, it is not necessary that the commitment be fully shared. There may be a partial but large area of agreement, and within that area theologizing may proceed, with speaker and listener in substantial and sympathetic collaboration. This is the advantage of the material which forms the subject matter of these pages. Practically all Christians and Jews will share my conviction that the Old Testament—the Jewish Scriptures—is in some sense the word of God, and that the history of the ancient people of Israel was God-guided in a way that is true of the history of no other nation.

The Old Testament itself contains material for a theology. That is, scientifically, by historical, literary, and doctrinal analysis, a body of doctrine and teachings concerning God can be educed from it. But although it contains some theological writing, taken as a whole it is not a work of theology: it is a work of history. This very peculiar feature of the Old Testament deserves to be stressed and brought out. It contains a story of divine activity, and yet it is not mainly, as are comparable narratives of the exploits of other gods, presented in mythological terms. It narrates God's deeds, as performed in the full light of human history and experience. They are witnessed to by flesh and blood men, men living similar lives to those of the narrators and recorders of the history. Geographically there is the same realism. The scenes of these actions are not some never-never land, the world of the gods, the recesses of the North, or some sacred and inaccessible domain belonging to God alone. No, the history is worked out on familiar ground: in the land of Egypt, in the Arabian desert, and above all in the valleys and on the hilltops, in the cities and in the villages, of Palestine. The greatest care is taken to link the events with places well known to the audience: with the ancient sanctuaries of Shechem, Bethel, Hebron, Beersheba; with the cities of Jerusalem, Tirsah, Hazor, Jericho; with the river Jordan and the Philistine cities on the coast; with the wells, the wadies, the groves, and the high places still part of the everyday life of the Israelite population. All this, in its way, is a denial of mythology. It expresses a vivid realism in the history, and an insistence that these events, thus pinned down and localized, are of another order than the recurring divine activity in the "natural forces" of the cosmos.

Thus the Old Testament—like the New for that matter —is no catechism, no textbook, no theological manual of timeless truths and abstract doctrine about the nature or attributes of the God it glorifies. On the contrary, it aims at being a sort of eyewitness account, a body of testimony to deeds done and victories accomplished by a real and personal divinity, who has performed his actions in the full sight of men.

This existential, realist approach is unique. The Koran has scraps of history in it, but formally it is a record of instruction and revelation received from the mouth of a divine messenger. Other sacred books narrate the doings and behavior of the gods on their home ground, so to speak, in a world outside time and space, as in a hundred different mythologies; or else they are historical, but centered on human figures, on the lives of holy men and religious heroes who have experienced a god in various ways, and have organized the results of their experience for the benefit of their fellows. But in the Hebrew Scriptures there is this extraordinary combination of historical realism and theocentrism. No man, and no series of men, makes up the central figure of this history. That figure is the deity himself. It has been well said there are no heroes in the

Old Testament, only weak, cunning, fragile men, visited from time to time by the spirit of God.*

Because the Israelites cast their doctrine, their experience of God, in historical form, that doctrine can be judged partly at least by historical methods; they appeal to history, and they must abide the judgment of history. Historical science nowadays possesses a very much more formidable and penetrating technique than anything known to the ancient or for that matter the medieval world. Every age has its own way of representing the past, of fixing it and mastering it and making it relevant to contemporary interests. Our approach in this matter is far removed from that of the ancient historiographers. Therefore, on the one hand, we must be careful not to be unfair to them by condemning them for not understanding history as we understand it; on the other hand, if their technique, within its own terms of reference, was valid and reliable, we should be able to restate the history in our terms and according to our categories and concepts.

Especially, it is possible now—it has become so within the last hundred years—to illuminate magnificently the background (as we consider it) of the Old Testament story. Instead of the spotlight falling on the sole figure of Israel, the lighting has spread to the whole scene, and we see that (in terms of external political history) Israel is practically an extra, a minor character, in a tableau where the center of the stage is held by the prestigious figures of Babylonia and Egypt, with many other important characters grouped around them. But—to pursue the metaphor —Israel is to be revealed at the end of the play as the unknown prince and hero, whose importance in reality outranks that of all the others.

However, for the first scenes it is highly profitable and instructive to devote some attention to these other characters. This is now possible, thanks primarily to the enormous modern development of the science and techniques of archaeology, which have restored to the light of day and

* C. Moeller, in "The Bible and Modern Man," *Lumen Vitae*, 10 (1955), p. 56.

to the consciousness of men literally dozens of dead civilizations, peoples, and literatures, long buried in the ground. The Sumerians, the early Akkadians, their successors the Babylonians, the fearsome Assyrians, the Hittites and all their associates, the Hurrians and the citizens of Mitanni in Upper Mesopotamia, the Aramaeans, the merchants of Ugarit and the Phoenician cities, the various Canaanite populations—with all of these the modern archaeologist or historian of the period has more than a nodding acquaintance, not only from the material remains of their temples, houses, and tombs, but, in most cases, from written records and literature. A brilliant and sophisticated international civilization flourished in the Near East in the Middle Bronze Age, that is, in the first half of the second millennium B.C., and the succeeding periods were scarcely inferior in social and political organization.

My interest here is not in the social organization, the political adventures, or the level of material comfort achieved by these groups. As Israel's history is entirely God-centered and religiously conditioned, my comparisons will be restricted as far as possible to the religious area. What were the religious wellsprings of these opulent civilizations? How did these peoples think of the gods whom they revered and served, and what sort of salvation did they look for? I have preferred to make that last question the central point of inquiry here. It will be found effective, I think, both in pinpointing the specific character of these different religions, and in bringing out the contrast between them and the religion of Israel.

Some doctrine of salvation belongs to every religion. If man feels himself dependent on a superhuman power, and endeavors to influence that power in his own favor, it is because man's desires, hopes, yearnings, outrun his own abilities. Salvation may be roughly defined as the good which men can imagine and desire but cannot surely achieve by their own unaided efforts. From the human point of view, one might say that gods exist in order to provide men with salvation. It is of course idle to try to distinguish what we now call temporal from eternal salvation. That is mainly a Christian distinction, and is unknown to the period we are dealing with.

Let us consider first the civilization of ancient Egypt. To make the main point at once: as an example of tenacious and successful conservatism, the Egyptian society is unrivaled in human history. Not even the rigid organization of ancient China so effectively held at bay, for so long a time, the change and decay that threaten all things human. For fully two thousand years, Egypt marshaled her resources and clung to her traditions, with the fierce determination not to let anything slip away from her, not to lose anything of the miraculously harmonious way of life that she had achieved, as at one stroke, at the very beginning of her history.

At first glance, this conquest of time, this defiance of mutability, has something about it almost awe-inspiring. At a closer look, however, the historian must note how artificial, even unreal, was much of this claimed fixity. There were two great periods in Egypt's history when the traditional structure of her society largely broke down, and after which the ancient hierarchy and social relationships had to be laboriously reconstructed. The first was the "First Intermediate Period," as it is called, which succeeded the collapse of the Old Kingdom, and lasted from about 2200 to 2000 B.C. The second was the period of domination by foreign rulers, the Hyksos, roughly from 1700 to 1550 B.C. Even the so-called heresy of Akhnaton (Amenophis IV), which attempted to suppress the worship of the ancient gods in favor of the sole worship of the sun-god Aton, though it lasted less than a century, was a drastic interruption of the rites and practices on which Egypt believed her wellbeing and survival to depend.

But besides these massive mutations—which in each case were ephemeral and were followed by a deliberate restoration of the old ways—there was, far more subtle and unremarkable, the steady process of evolution and development in social and religious thought, a process that eluded all checks and controls if only because it was imperceptible to the men who experienced it. Still, when these allowances have been made, we must marvel at the achievement of Egypt, the measure of success gained in this deliberate policy of "stopping the clocks." It can be seen, for instance, in the Egyptians' system of writing: the rhythmic and harmonious designs of the hieroglyphs which expressed their language underwent only minute variations from the Old Kingdom down to the Hellenistic age. Two other scripts, hieratic and demotic, were successively introduced to supplement this laborious sacred writing. But hieroglyphic itself was not allowed to evolve. The spoken language inevitably did so; even then, its phonetic changes developed much more slowly than we should expect from the analogy of our modern tongues. The same fixity, the same determination to resist change, is seen in their art, their burial customs, their rituals and liturgies, their literature, and practically every other department of their life.

Now this gives us an idea of what the Egyptians prayed for, what they desired from their gods. They wanted only more of the same. Life in the Nile Valley was a good life, and any change must be for the worse. History had no real meaning for them; existence was fixed in an unchanging rhythm of natural forces, to which they were well adjusted and which seemed incapable of improvement. There is a Christian formula which, applied strictly to the welfare of man and his harmony with the cosmos, rather neatly expresses the Egyptian outlook and hope: "As it was in the beginning, is now, and ever shall be, world without end." That was the business of the gods. Let them see to it that the Nile flowed regularly through the land, that it punctually and adequately rose in flood each summer, that the crops were abundant, that the north wind continued to blow, that the sun-god in particular made his daily majestic progress from east to west across the sky. Then the Egyptian knew that the gods were in their heaven, all was right with the world.

But what of the individual in his generation? And what of his personal salvation when his earthly life and breath departed from his body? Here the ancient Egyptian had a sublime confidence in the future state that awaited him.

As he resisted all change in life, so he minimized the change of death itself. But by a curious paradox, this people that sought to belittle death, to view it merely as a passage to a resumption on a higher level of the life they already knew, managed in doing so to give death an extraordinary prominence in their thoughts and activities. There is an amusing recognition of this in the reproach addressed by the Israelites to Moses in the Book of Exodus 14:11—"Were there no graves in Egypt, that you have led us away to die in the desert?" Egypt was above all the land of graves, the land of embalming and mummification, the land of elaborate funerals and mortuary rites, a land preoccupied with the service and glorification of the dead. The monuments that typify Egypt in everyone's mind, the very symbols of the permanence the Egyptians sought, the pyramids of Gizeh, are tombs.

The salvation desired by the Egyptian, then, was simply that this good life should continue indefinitely, eternally; and that he thought would be assured to him if his body lay undisturbed in its grave, if it was sufficiently incorrupt to supply a resting place for his soul, and if symbolic offerings of food were made available to it from time to time. It is true, there was also the uneasy idea that ethical righteousness in this life might have a bearing on continued happiness in the next. But, characteristically, that fear was dealt with by magical means. The dead man must be prepared to affirm his complete innocence, to deny absolutely any transgressions of moral or ritual norms; those disclaimers would be accepted at the judgment, and whatever his real behavior here on earth, he would be passed as fit for everlasting happiness.

Turning now to the other great ancient civilization that had influence in Israelite history, the Mesopotamian, we find ourselves in a very different atmosphere, a different culture, and especially a different world of religion. Materially, there were certain close parallels between Egypt and Babylonia. Both lands are river valleys, in which the rainfall is insignificant and of itself insufficient to support life (in Egypt rain is almost unknown; in Babylonia it averages less than ten inches a year). But the Nile in the west and the twin rivers of Tigris and Euphrates in the east provide abundant moisture, if men bestir themselves to make proper use of it. The Nile flood annually leaves a rich deposit of silt on the land for some miles on either side of the river, and the fields thus fertilized respond richly to cultivation. Tigris and Euphrates have a more even annual flow; moving sluggishly through the flat alluvial plain of Mesopotamia, they can be diverted and made to irrigate large areas of amazingly fertile soil. But this obviously requires human cooperation; the population must be organized and directed by a central authority, in order that canals may be dug, sluices constructed, channels dredged, and the life-giving waters fairly distributed to all the fields of a given community.

It was this successful human organization that lay at the basis of Mesopotamian cilivization. From small village units, with some democratic form of government, true urban communities developed. These populations, living in crudely fortified or at least enclosed cities, soon found it necessary, or advisable, to adopt monarchic rule. This transition to kingship, which must have occurred no later than the fourth millennium B.C., is always treated by the Babylonian historiographers as crucial, as marking the decisive step to truly civilized existence. Human society is constituted by it—the phrase they use to denote its beginnings is "The kingship was sent down from heaven"; that is, it was a gracious gift of the gods to mankind.

But the Babylonians were never as much at ease with their gods as were the Egyptians with theirs, and it is hard not to conclude that the sheer physical conditions of their lives had something to do with this. Nature (as we would call it) in Mesopotamia was much less indulgent to man than it was in Egypt—harsher, more erratic, less cooperative, and always threatening. The heat of the summer months was incredibly oppressive; sudden storms might demolish the mud-brick houses, break down the dikes, and flood the canals. Drought, or alternatively unseasonably heavy rains in the distant Armenian mountains, might allow river levels to sink to uselessness, or send the water suddenly flooding over newly planted fields.

Besides these material factors, a psychological one also came into play. The Babylonians, by comparison with their Egyptian contemporaries, appear to have been a dour and pessimistic lot. They took even their pleasures sadly; there was in their character, as recorded in their literature and art, a strain of savagery, combined with sensuality, at times both startling and repulsive. It was the Assyrians, after all, a northern tribe but also Semitic and akin to the Babylonians, who made brutality and calculated cruelty into a proclaimed policy of government.

The harshness of the Babylonian ethos is naturally reflected in the national religion; in fact it is concentrated there. The Babylonians transferred their own bitter struggle for existence and their inhumane treatment of enemies to their myths and cosmogonies. The establishment of order, the bringing of cosmos out of chaos, is pictured as a savage and merciless fight conducted between two groups of the gods. The leader of the forces of order, who successfully establishes the heavens and the earth, and sets in operation the universe as the Babylonians knew it, is (in the classical version of the story) Marduk, the patron god of Babylon. For this purpose complete power is made over to him by all the assembly of the gods—a mythological counterpart to the transition from democracy to kingship which had been judged necessary for the organization of human effort.

As for salvation, there was no question of a happy immortality after death. (The Egyptians were better off in both respects; they enjoyed this life, and were also serenely confident of happiness in the future.) Or rather, there was question of it, and the Babylonians answered the question firmly in the negative. Two or three of their myths picture an offer of immortality as being made to man; each time it is lost, not by man's fault but by the malice of some god or by sheer misfortune. The Epic of Gilgamesh, their most ambitious literary composition, is largely taken up with the hero's pursuit of immortality—which is finally and definitely in vain.

And all that man can look for is a modicum of physical enjoyment during this short life, a hope held out to Gilgamesh by the tavernkeeper in terms that curiously anticipate the Epicureanism of a later civilization, and even the measured judgment of Ecclesiastes:

> O Gilgamesh, where are you going?
> The life you are seeking you will never find.
> When the gods created mankind,
> death they allotted to man
> but life they kept in their own hands.
> You, Gilgamesh, fill your belly with good things,
> day and night rejoice . . .
> Look after the little one that takes your hand,
> let your wife be happy in your embrace;
> this is the lot of mankind.

Salvation was therefore limited to this life. But the Babylonian was by no means sure of obtaining it. His gods were always mysterious figures, unpredictable, touchy. They mirrored, after all, the natural forces of his environment—essentially, they were constituted as personifications of them—and as these forces operated erratically, unpredictably, and with an obvious disregard for man's convenience or well-being, so the Babylonian worshiper felt himself at a loss in trying to appraise the preferences, tastes, or demands of his gods. Obviously, they were to be fed, and they were to be served, and to both those duties he attended assiduously. But that was not enough. His conscience prescribed a certain moral code, and of that code, of justice between men, the gods were naturally thought to be guardians. Therefore they would punish unethical wrongdoing. But further, there was an extensive field of possible transgression that was nonmoral: the realm of taboos, of unlucky days, of arbitrary divine resentment. Hence the enormous development in Babylonia of superstition, of good-luck charms and talismans, of spells and incantations and magic of every variety. If the gods would not be reasonable, then they would have to be coerced into being cooperative. And that corruption of the religious instinct is, though not universal, frequently prominent in the texts of Babylonian rituals and prayers.

But a more personal, even affectionate, relationship to divinity was not unknown. The best of Babylonian religion comes out in the devotion to the family god or the personal god. The great gods who represented the cosmic powers of destiny, of fertility, of general well-being or the reverse, were officially and publicly worshiped in the city temples, by the city authorities. But presumably it was easy to think of them as too grand, too remote, and too preoccupied with large-scale affairs to be able to attend to the wants and troubles of the private individual. Hence the scene quite familiar in Babylonian iconography, especially in carvings on cylinder seals, of the worshiper being taken by the hand and introduced to the enthroned high god by his own personal patron and intercessor—his own family god. With such a god, if any, a man might have a personal relationship, might feel an intimacy given and returned such as he could never feel with the gods who presided over the universe.

Some few of the abundant prayers left to us in Babylonian literature illustrate such a relationship. I will quote one from the very end of this period, from a building inscription of the great Nebuchadnezzar who is so prominent in the stories of the Book of Daniel. The prayer is addressed to Marduk, the great patron of the city of Babylon and therefore the greatest of the gods. But in this case, since the suppliant is the king himself, he addresses his prayer to Marduk with the simplicity and initmacy proper in dealing with a personal god.

To Marduk my Lord I prayed. Prayers to him I made; the word which my heart sought, that I told him: "Apart from thee, O Lord, what would become of the king whom thou lovest, and whose name, well-pleasing to thee, thou didst pronounce? Do thou lead him aright; on the path of righteousness do thou direct him, since I am a prince and thy favorite, the creature of thy hand. It was thou that didst create me; thou didst entrust to me kingship over all peoples. In accordance with thy favor, O Lord, which thou hast bestowed on them all, make loving thy exalted lordship, and the fear of thy divinity implant in my heart. Grant me that which pleases thee, O thou who hast indeed created my life."

If anything strikes us about a prayer like that, it is that the god is ennobled by his client, rather than the reverse. Nothing is told us of Marduk elsewhere, in the mythology or in the form of any revelation or message, which demonstrates this character of benignity, righteousness and love for men, which Nebuchadnezzar here ascribes to him. It is a postulate of human devotion; but Marduk remained dumb. The priests of Babylon told stories about him; soothsayers would declare that such and such was his will; but his voice was never heard. He never issued forth as a complete personality, never stepped out of his function as patron and personification of the city, never really became more than a heavenly symbol of the earthly primacy of Babylon.

And that was the fate of Egyptian and Babylonian gods alike, and of many others whom I have not taken time to mention, those of the Canaanites, Assyrians, Hurrians, Hittites. They were inescapably relative, bound in their being as in their genesis to a given place or sector of human existence, or to a particular function or phenomenon of nature, never established as transcendent and self-sufficient. I have not mentioned the misty figures of the supposed high gods, whom some scholars consider to have deserved those epithets—for example, the supposed original high god of the Semites, El or Ilu. I note simply that such a divinity, at least in the historical period we are here concerned with, received no cult, was not considered as active or concerned about mankind, and therefore—to return to my starting point—was not a bringer of salvation. For that finally is the test: we are not finding fault with men, or condemning them for egoism, if we say that they will not serve a god who has nothing to offer them. If he is what he should be, then indeed, in the Christian phrase, to serve him is to reign; and the obligation to revere and worship him will coincide with man's own best interest and procure him the salvation of which he stands, helplessly, pitiably, in need. Neither the Egyptians nor the Babylonians encountered such divinities. It was reserved to another people, no more gifted and certainly no more deserving, to hear a God speak to them and offer them a salvation far beyond their wildest dreams.

# Chapter 2

## God: Power or Personality

IN THE PRECEDING PAGES we considered the quest for salvation in the ancient Near East, and some characteristic attitudes of men toward the gods. Taking the two great civilizations of Mesopotamia and Egypt in the second and first millennia B.C., we saw how their religions could in practice be understood and analyzed as a seeking after salvation, in the widest sense. The existence of gods and goddesses, of a superhuman world of knowledge and power, was completely unquestioned; the belief in such a world belonged to the fundamental categories of their thought, and was their frame of reference for all activity. But the practical question was, how could these superhuman beings be induced to exert themselves for the benefit of insecure and dependent mankind? How influence the gods—negatively, that they might not destroy or injure man; positively, that they might procure for him the salvation, that is, the desirable but inaccessible goods, of which he stood in need?

We saw that the gods were thought of as having charge of various sectors of the universe; either by appeasement and petition, or very often by magic and constraining spells, men sought to influence them and prevail upon them to grant the blessings which they seemed at times capriciously to withhold.

Here I shall develop somewhat the analysis of these ancient deities of polytheism, stressing an aspect of their natures in which they provide an instructive contrast with the God of the Old Testament, who is also the God of Christianity. For the comparison I shall take the concept of the Old Testament God, not in its full and late development, but as we can perceive it in the very first awareness of him that the Israelite tradition has preserved. The point of comparison is the question of personality as distinct from mere power. To what extent were the pagan deities thought of by their worshipers on the model of human persons? To what extent were they merely impersonal principles of action—that is, of power?

A preliminary remark is in place on the meaning of this distinction. On the principle of proceeding from the known to the unknown, concepts of divinity must be built up by men with the aid of images and concepts that derive from human experience, experience of themselves and their psychology, of the forces in their environment, of other animal or human beings. The Babylonian and Egyptian gods were originally thought of as the guiding and operating principles of what we should call the forces of nature. They were just sufficiently personalized or personified to enable them to be pictured as sacred or divine beings manifesting themselves in these forces. The Euphrates, for example, or the Tigris, was a god; the actual physical river, with all its power and size, its beneficial irrigation and its disastrous overflows, was the visible aspect of a divine being, who doubtless had his own plans and intentions, and was not necessarily concerned with the well-being and preferences of men. Similarly for the Egyptians, who felt their gods to be more kindly, the sun was the living symbol of Atum-Ra, the greatest of the gods, who daily traversed the land of Egypt dispensing health, fertility, and benediction to all the race of men, or at least to all the race of Egyptians. These natural objects, as we consider them, were not really worshiped in themselves, in their pure materiality; what were adored and invoked were the divinities of which they were the manifestations.

But such a particular divinity, thus equipped with a local habitation and a name, remained severely limited by the very nature of his function. One could describe him in terms of the river or the sun or whatever else he stood for; but his private life, if any, remained unknown. Calling something by a personal name and addressing it as "you" is not sufficient to give it the characteristics by which an actual living person would be identified and known. A person cannot be limited and defined merely in terms of a particular activity which he performs. He has his own existence, his unique history, his private interests, his character and potentialities. In short, he has his individual incommunicable personality, which is expressed in all his acts but not exhausted by all of them put together. Now these ancient polytheists presumably recognized this richness of personality in themselves and in one another; but they never succeeded in realizing it in their divinities. Their gods remained what they were to start with, personifications, or rather divinizations, of natural phenomena; they were never completely liberated from those phenomena, never persons in their own right. They could be, and were, presented as characters in stories, the myths, of which I shall speak later; but these succeeded only in giving them the traits of ordinary, sensual, violent men and women, without lending them distinctive and recognizable personalities. Some of them—Shamash the sun-god in Mesopotamia, Osiris in Egypt—were said to be guardians of morality, patrons of justice, vindicators of wrongdoing. They were praised, and prayed to, in those terms. But the stories told of them did not show them in any such noble light. Just as with the Olympian divinities of classical Greece, the gods and goddesses of Mesopotamia, in particular, might well be put to shame by any decent-living man or woman among their clients.

Thus, the encounter—what Martin Buber has called the "I-Thou" confrontation—was not really possible in Babylonian or Egyptian religion. We may admit that, subconsciously, religious-minded men and women yearned for it, as the intensely pleading tone of some of their prayers indicates, but there was no organ on the side of the gods, no voice of prophet or priest or oracle-giver, to make reply in the god's name in a correspondingly personal tone of voice. At most, there could be assurance of forgiveness, of prayers heard, of favorable omens, of a fortunate destiny. No doubt there was often the experience of a petition granted. By and large, these peoples made the best of the religion they had, and of the gods they knew; and only occasionally is there record of a pessimistic or skeptical thinker, expressing doubt or distrust concerning the fundamental justice of the gods and the meaning and value of human existence here on earth.

But if the concept of personality in the gods was feebly developed, and could never pass beyond a certain point, the concept of power in divinity was quite clear-cut and realistically grasped. It was by this, really, that the world of the gods was marked off from the world of men. To Babylonian and Egyptian alike the gods were mighty and all-powerful. In them collectively resided all imaginable power of action, and whatever abilities were innate in or acquired by men were simply communicated from on high. In the first place, to the gods were due the creation and the organization of the cosmos. In common with practically all peoples, Babylonia and Egypt had their myths of origin. These began usually by narrating the genesis of the gods themselves, which necessarily had to precede the genesis of the world; then, when the gods, or at least some generations of them, were in being, the myth would proceed to tell of their work of organizing the cosmos—distinguishing the regions of the universe, creating vegetation and animal life, and allotting these, usually, to the care of the appropriate divinities. Finally would come the formation and vivification of mankind.

Further, of course, the operation of the universe was cared for by the gods. The circling of the heavens, the yearly rhythm of the seasons, the regular movements of sun and moon, the flowing of the rivers—all these were maintained by the gods who personified these realities, and if they became negligent, or were angry with mankind, then these phenomena might be disturbed, or perhaps even cease altogether. The great and sacred mystery of fertility was the domain of the greatest gods. The maintenance, renewal, transmission of life was their supreme gift to men. The fruitfulness of the soil, the yields of wheat and barley, date palm and olive tree—these were supervised and nourished by the gods of vegetation. Similarly with the livestock, on which (from the modern point of view) both cultivation and transport largely depended—the cattle and goats which made up much of men's wealth, and the wild game which was hunted as an important supplementary food supply. Above all, human fertility was the one most sought-after blessing. It could be obtained only from the gods of generation and sex. One might remark in passing that the specter of overpopulation never entered the wildest dreams of these ancient peoples. The more offspring the better; the more numerous the family or people, the more strength it had, the more secure it was against its enemies, the more resources were at hand to exploit the gods' bounty. (In only one respect, perhaps, was the desire for offspring qualified—in the lukewarm attitude to the birth of daughters. But of sons, a man or a city or a people could never have too many.)

Those then were the functions, that was the character, of the gods of the ancient world. Founded on men's conviction of the existence of superhuman powers, they were specified and individualized according to the areas of the natural world that concerned man's existence, and imperfectly personified after the image of man's own consciousness. From them, the people of Babylonia and Egypt ardently but uncertainly sought the fulfillment of their cravings, and the accomplishment of their salvation.

Now, if we turn to the Israelite tradition, at the earliest moment at which it is accessible to us, we find even at that starting-off point a very instructive contrast. The men who are here in question belong certainly to the Babylonian culture; their sociological setting, their legal practices and customs, their outlook and mentality are already familiar, and in conformity with the Mesopotamian civilization of the Middle Bronze Age. But the nature of the divinity whom they encountered and the relationship of this particular god to these particular men represent something that the biologist would call a mutation. There is an abrupt discontinuity, which clearly implies the intrusion of some new and unprecedented factor.

The stage at which I am considering the emergence of this new religious vision—for it is that—is found in the traditions concerning Abraham, preserved to us by a long process of transmission, compilation, and editing, in the present text of the Book of Genesis. This text has been established and practically immune to change since at least the fourth century B.C.; and the traditions it contains have, in part, been fixed in their present wording since at least the tenth century B.C. It would be out of place here to go into a discussion of the literary and historical problems connected with these and other Old Testament traditions. Fortunately, these problems are largely irrelevant to the argument. One is on safe ground in maintaining that Abraham was a historic individual, that, as head of a clan, he did migrate from Upper Mesopotamia to the land of Canaan, and that he believed he was doing so under the protection, and with the approval, of a particular god. So far there is nothing that could not be predicated of a score of other seminomad groupings that were on the move in the same general area in the Middle Bronze Age. We cannot date these events very precisely; between the nineteenth and seventeenth centuries B.C. is as close as we can come.

But that bare statement of a move from one part of the Fertile Crescent to another would be a totally insignificant historical fact, were it not for the religious experience that accompanied it. Theologically, it appears as the decisive event in all that ancient history. Even the secular historian must reckon with it, because of the influence it exerted on subsequent human behavior. For the Christian or Jewish theologian, it is the starting point of divine revelation in the wide sense, an initial act of God in the great drama of salvation.

Again, we need not trouble to draw fine distinctions between the event as understood by contemporaries, including Abraham himself, and the event as interpreted by the people who looked back on him as their father. To the latter, its significance had undoubtedly become clearer and more explicit. In a long process of oral transmission, the narratives were stripped down to their essentials, and many of the multifarious details of the original experience were dropped off and forgotten. Conversely, the radical religious symbolism was heightened and more clearly brought out by various narrative devices, such as theophanies and divine speeches. But this was only a matter of selection and emphasis. The religious significance must have been inherent in the events from the start; that is, it must have been, however dimly, experienced by the human participants at the time. After all, we have to put this mutation, the emergence of this new concept of divinity, somewhere in history; and if we reject the point to which it is clearly ascribed by tradition, then we shall simply have to postulate, arbitrarily, some later breakthrough, of which we have no evidence at all. Sound methodology requires that we work with the materials we have. Of course, we must still use critical judgment, in attempting to separate the nucleus of the original experience from the developments superimposed by the faith of later generations.

Now it is a priori morally certain that a new departure by a seminomad group, a striking out in a new direction in search of fresh pasturage, or different social relationships, would be an act religiously conditioned and would need divine sanction. I mean, in the concrete, that if conditions of overcrowding, exhausted food supply, or perhaps political insecurity and excessive brigandage made it imperative for a seminomad family to seek some new and unfamiliar area, where it could hope to flourish and expand, then both the area to be chosen, and the precise time and route for setting out, would be referred to a divinity for determination and approval. No Semite of the second millennium B.C. could dream of such a radical change of living, unless he secured assurance of divine help and protection in his enterprise.

With this in mind we may examine the tradition recorded in Genesis; its first occurrence will give us the substance of the story.

Yahweh said to Abram, "Set out from your native land, from your people and from your family, towards the land which I will show you. I will make you into a great nation. I will bless you, and make your name so great it will be a source of blessing. I will bless those who bless you and those who curse you I will curse. And all the families of the earth will bless themselves by you." (Gen. 12:1–3.)

Now, in accord with what was just said, we may note that this statement need not exclude tangible and practical reasons why Abraham should have been thinking of moving, anyway. This divine oracle could quite well be a response to a consultation or inquiry. We do not know. The decisive thing, in any case, is the divine answer which sanctioned and directed the move. And already here we can measure the vast difference which separates this from divine response or commands in any religion of the time.

In the first place there is a direct person-to-person meeting. Abraham is addressed as "thou" and the god speaks as "I." There is a confrontation, and a purpose and an intention are communicated by one party to the other. This god has a plan, a program, involving this man and his whole race. Yet it is not a mere proclamation or prediction. The man's response and cooperation are required. That is, the god is a person and he treats Abraham as a person. The latter is not merely a client, a customer, or a suppliant. Much less is he merely a servant or a slave. The Koran as well as the Old Testament gives Abraham an expressive title, *Khalil Allah,* "the friend of God"; and that is what is implied here. Abraham's dignity is recognized, his self-determination respected, by his being taken into a species of partnership. He is invited to cooperate with the plan of this god.

Further, the plan is, apparently, entirely for Abraham's benefit. No indication is given that the god is to get anything out of it, unless it be, eventually, a more extended worship from the multitude of Abraham's descendants. Divine messages and instructions are recorded in much of Near Eastern history, but their beneficiary normally is to be the god himself. Man can at most expect a certain reward for giving the god what he wants. Thus with the dreams of Gudea, Sumerian Prince of Lagash in the twenty-first century B.C., who was instructed to erect a new temple to Ningirsu. Thus with the instructions to later Assyrian monarchs, who were ordered to carry devastation far and wide, as a means of glorifying the power of Assur.

Again, this command is a specific one. It is not to be understood as though, in general, the will of this god is that all city dwellers should disperse into the wilderness, or that all the nomads around Haran should move in the direction of Canaan. On the contrary, tribe and clan are to be left behind; they are to remain in the land; and Abraham alone is picked out for a peculiar and mysterious destiny.

This destiny is one of salvation, and it is expressed in terms of the well-being that is desired by the sheep nomads of the time—the only terms, presumably, that a man like Abraham would understand and appreciate. These seminomads had achieved an internally well-adjusted way of life, which nevertheless was externally a precarious one, subject to all kinds of hazard and interference. A patriarchal family was really a tribe in miniature. It might include dozens of adults, scores of slaves, hundreds of children, and flocks and herds numbered in the tens of thousands. All this was its wealth; but the latter's conservation and increase depended on the control of seasonal resources of water and pasturage, on defense against marauders, and on a friendly and peaceable relationship with cities and settled areas in whose environs the group had to exist. Given these conditions, the family would expand indefinitely, and that was the salvation, the blessing, for which it sought the aid of its gods. In such growth, the head of the family, the patriarch or sheik, grew and flourished, and eventually enjoyed a vicarious but true and much coveted immortality, in the numerous descendants who bore his name.

There is more than that. The promise that "all the families of the earth" would bless themselves by Abraham has been taken as meaning no more than that he would become a proverbial example of the happiest man that ever lived. But this is a quite inadequate understanding of the very concrete meaning that is attached to ancient blessings. If people are to bless themselves through (or in or by) Abraham, this has to mean that somehow Abraham's blessing is communicated to them. To some degree, therefore, he will be multiplied not only in his bodily descendants, the people who take their origin from him, but in all the families of the earth. The old translation, "In you shall all the families of the earth be blessed," was grammatically less accurate; but in substance it expresses exactly what the original implies.

This sweeping promise, finally, tells us much about the god who makes it. And here we come to the central points, which are also the most delicate. What is the character of this god? What is his origin? What was Abraham's relation to him?

We have just seen that he can make a promise involving the whole of mankind. This element may well have been less prominent in the original event than it now appears. Yet it must have been present then. Such universalism was by no means common or fundamental in the religion of Israel itself, until the postexilic age. It is hard to imagine its being inserted into the tradition concerning Abraham at any time between Moses and the Exile. In its present form, the passage we are dealing with is definitely pre-exilic. Therefore the most plausible supposition is still that the God of Abraham, even at the time the tradition was formed, was regarded as enjoying unrestricted freedom of action, both at the contemporary moment and for all time in the future, and that his plan of bestowing salvation was framed so as to extend eventually to all mankind. This is not, of course, a denial of the existence or reality of other gods. At most, it implies that they would be unable to interfere with this god's project and activity.

Now, for the other half of this dialogue, I may join here an item from the Elohist version of the call of Abraham, in Genesis 15:

Yahweh led him outside, and said, "Look up at the sky, and see if you are able to count the stars. Just so numerous," he said to him, "shall your descendants be." Abram believed Yahweh; and Yahweh credited it to him as justice.

This is the famous faith of Abraham, unendingly praised by the later tradition, and by St. Paul. He is presented for all time as the model of commitment, the exemplar of right response on the part of man the creature to the personal invitation of God the creator. But I am concerned for the moment with the original bearing of this attitude of trust which is so praised, because it may throw some light on the historical event, on the beginning and early development of Abraham's commerce with this god. Faith is the assurance of what we hope for, our conviction about things we cannot see, we are informed in Hebrews. And if Abraham's trust in this divine promise is something deserving of mention and so much stressed by the tradition, this seems to imply that he had so far had little or no experience of this god's saving power.

If we seek some kind of precedent (though it will not be very close) in Babylonian religious beliefs and practices for Abraham's experience, the only plausible one will be the devotion to a personal god. As was mentioned in the previous chapter, the one place where the Babylonians came close to a truly personal relationship in prayer was in the individual's private devotion to his own special divinity, who was his particular intercessor with the great gods. Even there, the personal note was one-sided; the god's response was perceived rather in what he was thought to do than in anything he was reported to have said. There is no record of a direct, arbitrary, mysteriously forward-looking combination of command and promise such as the first passage cited from Genesis. But if such an invitation, containing a promise of salvation, were to be forthcoming to a private citizen of Babylonian culture, then it would be comprehensible only as a personal message directly communicated from his personal god.

Another similarity between "the God of Abraham" and

the personal gods of Babylonia consists in the former's complete detachment from particular places and circumstances. He is pictured as indifferent to conditions and techniques of revelation or communication. Sometimes he manifests himself to Abraham at sanctuaries—Shechem, Bethel, Hebron—but these holy places are alike as far as he is concerned: his choice is determined practically, one would say, by the hazard of Abraham's wanderings. Sometimes he appears in broad daylight; sometimes, in the night, whether in dream or in waking vision. Sometimes he uses the intermediary of messengers; at other times, he walks and talks with Abraham *in propria persona*, and once at least he accepts a meal, and eats and drinks while Abraham serves him. This great variety of manifestation is assembled, it is true, from the various forms the traditions have assumed in the course of transmission (particular collections of material, such as the Yahwist or the Elohist, may be more limited and consistent in their portrayal of theophanies); but this variation at least shows the consistency in these matters was thought to be a matter of indifference to this god. Here he contrasts notably with the Babylonian deities, who were specialists even in their oracle-giving. Each had his favorite temple, his special staff of priests and soothsayers, and his preferred technique of consultation—incubation in temples, drawing of lots, consulting of beasts' livers, observation of oil on water or of flights of birds, etc. But Abraham's God is unlimited, in this as in other ways.

This god then is identified simply as the God of Abraham, and he gives a command and makes a promise which are far-reaching indeed. They express his all-sufficiency, his ability to take the place of all other gods where Abraham is concerned, in any part of the world to which Abraham travels. The patriarch is to abandon his entire social setting, the security and support of kinsfolk that he has so far depended on; and this implies also the abandonment of reliance on any other gods, whether local or even ancestral. Further, this god is (to put it in modern terms) one who controls history; he is not limited to maintaining a *status quo*. He has a plan and a destiny for Abraham which he intends to accomplish in his own good time. That is, he not only has power which is unconfined, unrivaled, indefinitely great. He has also a mind of his own, he takes an initiative, he announces a purpose. For the first time, a god comes forward as a person.

Inevitably, as I have already allowed, the story of Abraham and his mysterious vocation has been colored and edited by later generations, in the light of what they considered the fulfillment of this plan and promise. Abraham's own theology, his religion and his concept of this personal god, was no doubt extremely rudimentary and crude, if compared with, say, the theology of the prophets. But, for reassurance that the editing of the stories has not gone very far, that the tradition is substantially untampered with, we may turn our attention to the things it does *not* say. In the earlier versions of the tradition, in Genesis 12 and 15, this god is not limited by any qualification. He is not presented as a creator-god, or as a sky-god, or as a supreme god of any kind. Nothing is said of any connection he may have with the origins or maintenance of the universe. His relationship to the deities of other countries and peoples is not made clear (we see only, in the story of Abraham in Egypt, that this god deals as he pleases with the great Pharaoh of Egypt himself, and that the gods of Egypt have nothing to say). Nothing is stated about his possible connection with other men besides Abraham and his descendants, apart from what is implied by the one reference to "all the families of the earth." Similarly this god has no territorial bonds—though he can apparently choose and assign to Abraham any country that he pleases, regardless of the people and the gods that now inhabit it. In short, if there is one specification, it is only that he is a god of salvation. He promises to Abraham a destiny and an immortality such as men might dream of but hardly dare to seek; and even in making that promise he demonstrates indirectly that he has the power that is needful to fulfill it. It was under this formality of salvation that the God of Israel first presented himself to a man.

The development of this encounter and the further acquaintance with Abraham's God make up the rest of the Old Testament, and are prolonged in Christianity. But the uniqueness of this idea of God is perhaps best perceived by the historian in this tradition of its very beginning, the bare statement of a theophany and a divine initiative, so concisely and baldly narrated, yet implying so much. Against the Near Eastern background, especially of Mesopotamian religion and life, its novelty is unmistakable. The details of the patriarchal narratives in the following chapters of Genesis, the laws of inheritance and of marriage in particular, are in conformity with Mesopotamian customs and the famous code of Hammurabi (and incidentally quite different from the law of Moses and the later customs of Israel). All the more clearly do we perceive the new departure in religion, when a truly personal God makes himself known to the man of his choice.

# Chapter 3

## Israel's Covenant with God

IN THE PREVIOUS CHAPTER I drew a comparison, which turned into a contrast, between the normal concept of divinity in the polytheist religions of the ancient Near East, and the concept of the personal and unlimited God so firmly and consistently presented in the traditions about Abraham. The latter appears curiously distinctive, in fact unique. Personality, vividly realized, is the mark of Abraham's God, and he is quite independent of, in fact he transcends, the various special functions and activities to which the other gods are dedicated.

I now come to speak of the divine image, the concept of the divinity, as it occurs in the Old Testament tradition regarding Israel's own origin. This people's literature centered precisely on the activity of their God; and one of his most striking achievements was that he had created and constituted the people, not in any dim mythical past, but at a specific and well-remembered time, at a period in history when other nations and peoples and civilizations were already ancient and long-established. Israel was not, even in its own eyes, an aboriginal population, sprung from the earth as the first fruits of divine creative activity. On the contrary, the Israelites were latecomers on the world's stage, and they were there at all only because a certain God had chosen to create them.

It is interesting to observe the parallel between Abraham's experience and Israel's. Spontaneously, and I am sure unconsciously, the masters of tradition in Israel, the priests and teachers and early prophets, exposed exactly the same sort of activity in the latter case as in the former, because in each the same God was at work, with the same unique personality and characteristics. Thus, his call to Abraham is gratuitous, a free initiative owing nothing to human factors; and so is his choice of Israel, and his intervention on behalf of this people. He leads Abraham out of his human setting and way of life, detaches him from reliance on kinsfolk and familiar society; similarly, he insists on bringing Israel out of Egypt, uprooting these Hebrews from the settled existence they have known, and launching them on a strange, wandering adventure, whose destination is his choice and whose duration depends on him. He establishes a special relationship between Abraham and himself, allowing himself to be identified as "the God of Abraham"; a special relationship is likewise set up in the covenant which makes Israel uniquely his people. Finally, in each case there is the aspect of promise, the commitment to a future good, implying this God's full control of history, his ability to mold and guide the destinies of men, and to achieve whatever consummation he desires.

There is, however, one important difference in these two relationships, of Abraham with his God and of Israel with hers; it is psychological, and it lies in the different natures and reactions of the human partners concerned. Abraham —and the same applies in large measure to Isaac, to Jacob, and to Joseph—is shown as entirely responsive and loyal to the divine call. In other respects these patriarchs, in the traditions, are no plaster saints. They have the naive religious outlook of their time. Their religion retains a good deal of the bargaining attitude, they are cunning and childish at the same time, they coax and wheedle and haggle with God. They are at ease with him; but, also, they have the naive trust of children, and they conform themselves entirely to his good will and pleasure, as far as these are understood. The most striking case here is that of Jacob, the least admirable though not the least interesting of these characters. Jacob is in some ways contemptible: he is calculating, self-interested, and unscrupulous; but his life is a long history of discipline, chastisement, and purification by affliction. Not one of his misdeeds is left unpunished; the law of talion operates, set in motion by his own wrongdoing. But throughout he is being chastened by the hand of that same God, and to him he is always grateful and loyal.

Not so with Israel as a people. In their historic period, when all these traditions were collected and arranged, and treasured as the records of the great deeds of their God, they looked back on the patriarchs as their ancestors, indeed, yet as distinct from themselves. Whereas, with the generation to whom Moses spoke, they felt full identity. That *was* Israel, and the keen consciousness of solidarity and union between successive generations meant that the Israelites of the tenth, eighth, or sixth centuries B.C. felt themselves entirely one with the motley crowd that had departed out of Egypt. This is the Deuteronomic doctrine: Israel is one and indivisible, then and now; the speeches, promises, warnings spoken at Sinai or in Moab are addressed equally to each subsequent generation. The Israelites did not glorify themselves, as they could glorify the patriarchs. Inescapably, they had a sense of guilt as regards their defective response to God's message and demands; and they felt that their moral inadequacy, their infidelity, had existed from the very beginning. This is the main difference in the portrait of God sketched in the Book of Exodus, over against that of the second half of Genesis: he is much sterner, more awe-inspiring, more terrible in his condemnation of wrongdoers and his vindication of his demands. The difference really is not in him, however, but in the human material he is dealing with.

Parenthetically, I would draw attention here to yet another unique distinction of this literature of ancient Israel. It is a national literature that does *not* glorify the nation. There is no parallel that I have ever heard of to this phenomenon. Every other literature of a people, every collection of folklore, ballads, legend, or saga, in which a national consciousness has expressed and fixed the remembered history of a race, praises and magnifies that race, flatters the national ego, sets up an image with which each succeeding generation is proud and happy to identify itself. If the gods are brought into the history as saviors and patrons, then the glory of the people and the glory of its gods are one and the same.

Not so with Israel. "Not unto us, O Lord, but unto thy name give the glory." With extraordinary consistency and heroic honesty, Israel glorifies its God at the cost of belittling itself. He is always right, always holy, and greatly to be praised; and Israel his beneficiary has never perfectly responded, never been worthy of him, never given him back the obedience and gratitude that he had a right to expect.

I must here survey very briefly what can be determined of the historical background of the origins of Israel as a people. Again, the general outline can be sufficiently described from the traditions as preserved to us. We are shown a Semitic seminomad population of herdsmen and shepherds, occupying an area of fertile grazing land in the eastern Nile delta, the famous land of Goshen. They are aliens on Egyptian territory, and they remember that their ancestors migrated thither from Canaan. If, as is plausible, we associate that migration and arrival with the so-called Hyksos domination in Egypt, its rule by Semites in the seventeenth and sixteenth centuries B.C., then the so-called oppression to which the Hebrews were subjected would come under the vigorous native Pharaohs of the eighteenth dynasty, in the fourteenth and early thirteenth centuries.

These descendants of the Canaanites were not much Egyptianized. They had lived isolated from Egyptian life, retaining their own Semitic dialect, their own customs and rudimentary social organization. Their religion was presumably some form of Canaanite polytheism. Nowhere is there any hint that they knew or worshiped God who was to reveal himself to Moses; the tradition in Exodus 2 and 3 carefully avoids saying that they cried out *to him*. Yet in some groups at least there must have endured some traditions about Abraham and his God, and some memory of the promise. More than that we cannot attribute to these Hebrew tribes in Egypt; it is even an anachronism at this stage to call them Israelite; the people of Israel did not yet exist.

Against that background we can set the emergence of the figure of Moses—a man of Semitic race, belonging to this subject people, but of Egyptian training and education. This last is sufficiently evinced by his name, which is thoroughly Egyptian though abbreviated by dropping off the original Egyptian divine title. It is of the same type as the Pharaonic names of Ra-meses and Tut-moses, which mean "the god Ra or Toth has begotten (a son)." The legends about Moses' infancy and youth embody traditions of his Hebrew origin, his Egyptian training, his loyalty to his own people, his preparation for his work, and finally (a familiar symbolic theme) his retreat into the desert. He is driven out of his normal setting and retires to a hidden life—where finally the call of God comes to him.

This theophany, in Exodus 3 and 6, is crucial; and it shows the same elements of divine initiative, beneficence, and will that we have noted before. Further, there is the communication of a special name by which this God, who identifies himself with the traditional God of Abraham, is to be invoked. The name is mysterious, and its function is to reveal and conceal at the same time. It is possible, as many historians would hold, that Moses had learned it elsewhere, that a God Yahweh had already been invoked and worshiped by one of the groups that was to make up the people; but what is decisive and new is the image now evoked by it, the concept of the personality of the God who hereby announces to Moses his will to save this people, and Moses' function as his instrument.

The narrative of how the first stages of that plan were carried out must be summarized very briefly. We may note the stress on Yahweh's all-sufficiency. Men in general are uncooperative or they actively resist his will. The Pharaoh refuses to let the Hebrews depart, his magicians try to rival the powers given to Moses, the Hebrews themselves find this deliverance more than they bargained for, even Moses protests and begs off. But Yahweh's will is irresistible. All opposition is beaten down, and this mixed multitude, as the tradition calls it, this amalgam of Semitic serfs, nomads, and fugitives, finds itself, in despite of all the power of the greatest state of the time, mobilized and led into the desert. The Hebrews safely cross the water barrier that marks the eastern boundary of Egypt, an Egyptian detachment sent to round them up meets with disaster, and with mixed feelings of exaltation and un-easiness they are launched on their great adventure, on their divinely guided pilgrimage.

But their relationship to this divinity has still to be regularized and made official. So far, they have known him by the instructions Moses brought, and have experienced him as mysterious and omnipotent in the work of their liberation; but in the desert, at his chosen dwelling place, there is to be a meeting and the making of a covenant.

With this word "covenant" we come to one of the central concepts of the Israelite and indeed of the whole Judeo-Christian tradition. If we distinguish in the Christian Bible Old and New Testaments, that is only a variant expression for old and new covenants. The word is specific and distinctive.

Covenant—*berith* in Hebrew—was already a highly important sociological element in the life of the time, and it continued to be important for many centuries to come. *Berith* was a pact, a treaty, which established a permanent relationship between two or more originally unconnected parties. They might be two men, two families, two peoples. They might be a king and his subjects; they might be a group of individuals, or of social units such as tribes. The relationship established was equivalent to the closest possible natural bond. The parties obliged themselves, under penalty of curse and destruction, to be loyal and faithful to one another, to assist and support one another according to need and capability. There was a special word for the activity expected of a covenant partner: *hesed*. Though impossible to translate adequately, since it combines the ideas of love, loyalty, and ready action, and implies an existing covenant, it may be rendered "loving kindness," or perhaps better "covenant love."

In the historical traditions, we hear for instance of a Canaanite king Abimelek, who seeks and is granted a covenant with Isaac in order that he may benefit by the blessing and the extraordinary divine assistance that accompany the patriarch. In the narratives of David's early life, we see him and Jonathan conclude a personal covenant which binds each to loyal and loving support of the other. Many other examples are recorded. But interestingly enough, the closest parallel in terms and effects to the covenant at Mount Sinai has been uncovered only in modern times, through the work of the archaeologists who have excavated the ancient capital of the Hittite kingdom in modern Turkey, and have gathered and deciphered the archives of that long-forgotten civilization. It is the suzerainty treaties, as they are called, made by the great king of the Hittites with vassal princes in northern Syria, that furnish the most illuminating parallels to the covenant on which was based the religious existence of Israel.

The Hittite empire, from which these treaties come, is dated to the fourteenth and thirteenth centuries B.C., and is thus approximately contemporaneous with the origins of Israel. It is not to be supposed, of course, that Moses or any other Israelite leader knew the precise terms of these documents; rather, the latter are samples of the standard international treaty convention of the period, which, like the rest of the diplomatic procedures of the time, depended on Babylonian inventions. Treaties were later imposed on their subjects by Assyrian overlords in the ninth to seventh centuries B.C., but by that time the formula had changed, and the texts no longer show such striking similarities of content and expression with the Mosaic covenant.

The nature of these Hittite suzerainty treaties has been well analyzed by Professor Mendenhall:

The primary purpose of the suzerainty treaty was to establish a firm relationship of mutual support between the two parties (especially military support), in which the interests of the Hittite sovereign were of primary and ultimate concern. It established a relationship between the two, but in its form it is unilateral. The stipulations of the treaty are binding only upon the vassal, and only the vassal took an oath of obedience. Though the treaties frequently contain promises of help and support to the vassal, there is no legal formality by which the Hittite king binds himself to any specific obligation. Rather, it would seem that the Hittite king by his very position as sovereign is concerned to protect his subjects from claims or attacks of other foreign states. Consequently for him to bind himself to specific obligations with regard to his vassal would be an infringement upon his sole right of self-determination and sovereignty. A most important corollary of this fact is the emphasis upon the vassal's obligation to *trust* in the benevolence of the sovereign.*

Six main elements can be distinguished in the texts of most of these Hittite treaties.

1. A preamble which identifies the author of the covenant, giving his titles, attributes, and genealogy. For instance: "Thus speaks X, the great king, king of the Hittite land, son of Y, the valiant, the great king." Here emphasis is laid on the majesty and power of the king who is conferring a special relationship on the vassal.

2. A historical prologue which describes in detail the previous relations between the two parties. It outlines the benevolent deeds which the king has already performed for the vassal, not vaguely, but very specifically and factually. The implication is that the vassal is already obligated to the great king because of the favor and protection experienced in the past. Thus there is a real mutuality of contract; but the vassal is pledging future obedience and loyalty in return for past benefits which he received without having any claim to them. Strict obligation is on his side; on the great king's, there is no

* George E. Mendenhall, *Law and Covenant in Israel and the Ancient Near East* (Pittsburgh: The Biblical Colloquium, 1955), p. 30.

obligation other than the presumption and implied promise that he will continue his benevolence.

Notable is the personal form of this prologue. The great king addresses the vassal directly: "I have sought after you; although you were sick and ailing I put you in the place of your father and made your brothers and sisters and the whole Amurru country subject to you."

3. The stipulations which spell out in detail the obligations accepted by the vassal. These usually include:

    a. Prohibition of service to any other great king.

    b. Promise to be on friendly terms with the king's other vassals; if disputes arise they are to be submitted to the overlord's arbitration.

    c. Promise to send contingents to support the great king when he goes to war.

    d. Promise to trust the great king completely, and not to tolerate rebellious or critical language.

    e. Promise to bring yearly tribute in person, and on that occasion to renew fealty.

4. A directive that the treaty be deposited in the temple of the vassal city, and periodically read in the hearing of the people.

5. The invocation of the gods both of the Hittites and of the vassal as witnesses to the treaty.

6. Finally, the pronunciation of curses upon the vassal if he breaks the covenant, and the promise of blessings for its observance. These are the only sanctions expressly mentioned; that is, the Hittite king does not threaten military proceedings and destruction. The treaty is a sacred document, and it is the gods who will see to its enforcement and vindication.

So far the texts of these historical documents. As Professor Mendenhall points out, we must suppose—what is not recorded—that there was a solemn religious ceremony at the covenant making, in which the vassal swore to observe the terms of the covenant and invoked the curse of the gods on himself if he did not fulfill his oath. The yearly reading of the terms of the covenant, as we saw, was expressly prescribed.

Now let me briefly draw the parallels between this concept and that which underlies the traditions about the Mosaic covenant making as they are recorded in the Book of Exodus. It is fairly clear, and generally admitted, that the union of the tribes belonging to the Israelite federation —as we see them operating for instance in the period of the Judges, in the twelfth century B.C.—was religious rather than merely political; and it is a union not explicable merely by factors of geography or racial origin. The Israelite tribes of that period and of the later monarchy "were not an ethnically homogeneous group derived from a common ancestor, nor did Israel grow merely by biological reproduction."* Different groups of the population of Palestine (and earlier, perhaps other nomadic groups that the Hebrews encountered in their wanderings) must have entered en bloc into the federation of the traditional twelve tribes. From this point of view, the picture of twelve tribes in Egypt as all physically descended from one man, then moving as a unit from Egypt to Palestine, and there occupying the land under the sole leadership of Joshua is a legitimate but considerable simplification, a schematization, of the historical reality, which as always was complicated to a degree. In other words, the unity of the Israelites was a factitious one, which must have had its beginning on one definite historical occasion, and which supposes the intervention of some outstanding personality. One might say, in the light of the later history, that if Moses did not exist we should have to invent him. If we had no tradition about his covenant making, we should still be forced, in order to account for the later history of Israel, to postulate that something of the kind occurred.

We can identify at least a major part of the text of the covenant treaty, though in slightly modified form, in the Book of Exodus, chapter 20. It is remarkable that Moses is the intermediary but is not himself a partner to the covenant. The tribes do not swear allegiance to him. The

* *Ibid.*, p. 36.

treaty is being made between Yahweh as overlord and the collected tribes as his covenant partner, his vassals. The text contains the identification of the suzerain: "I am Yahweh thy God." Then comes the historical prologue, which establishes the obligation of Israel to its benefactor by briefly mentioning the previous relationship of the two parties, namely, the deliverance from Egypt: "who brought thee out of the land of Egypt, out of the state of bondage." And then follow the stipulations, the conditions which the suzerain imposes on his vassals and which the latter solemnly swear to observe. These of course are no other than the familiar Ten Commandments, a little code of religious and social law, later to be much expanded into the various other law codes of Israel. It begins, "Thou shalt not have other gods apart from me"; then there follows, "Thou shalt not carve thyself a statue," "Thou shalt not abuse the name Yahweh," and so on.

The requirement of conservation of the text and periodic public reading is not now attached to these stipulations; but we do have elsewhere the tradition about the inscribed stone tablets being preserved in the portable sanctuary, the ark of the covenant, and the periodic reading of the law is often insisted on. There naturally could be no list of gods as witnesses—it would be impossible to appeal to any third party as a guarantor of the treaty between Yahweh and Israel. But the formula of curses and blessings, not now attached to the Decalogue, is nevertheless an important and early part of the legal tradition. It concludes both the book of the covenant (Ex. 23) and the code of Deuteronomy (Deut. 28).

Further, in Exodus 24 we have a tradition about the actual covenant-making ceremony, which pictures it as accompanied by a communion sacrifice. First an altar is built and a victim prepared. Then the terms of the pact are read out, and the people answer, "All the rules that Yahweh has given we will observe." The victim is slaughtered; and Moses takes half of its blood and sprinkles it on the altar—which symbolizes the deity—and the other half he sprinkles on the twelve stone pillars that symbolize the tribes, saying, "Behold the blood of the covenant which Yahweh has made with you."

Thus it is reasonable to conclude to some connection between this form of suzerainty treaty, known to us from Hittite sources, and the almost contemporary form of covenant adopted by Moses to express the relationship which should henceforth bind this collection of tribes and clans to the service of their peculiar God. To quote Professor Mendenhall again:

the covenant form itself furnished at least the nucleus about which the historical traditions crystallized in early Israel. It was the source of the "feeling for history" which is such an enigma in Israelite literature. And perhaps even more important is the fact that what we now call "history" and "law" were bound up into an organic unit from the very beginnings of Israel itself. Since the cultus was at least connected with the covenant proclamation or renewal, we can see that in early Israel, history, cultus, and "law" were inseparable, and that the history of Israelite religion is not the history of the gradual emergence of new theological concepts, but of the separation and re-combination of these three elements so characteristic of Israelite religion, over against the mythological religions of their pagan neighbors.*

One aspect of this association of history, cultus, and law deserves comment. The stipulations of the covenant naturally had the function of laws, the first written laws, presumably, that the tribes had known up to that point. But the inclusion of law in the covenant formula meant that the very concept of law was changed. Law and jurisprudence had been highly developed for centuries in Mesopotamia—the great code of Hammurabi was drafted four centuries before Moses—but they had persistently maintained a nonreligious and profane character. The point may be demonstrated by reference to a typical example of the Babylonian legal formula: "If a man has

* *Ibid.*, p. 44.

killed a fellow citizen, he shall be put to death." The prescription is juristic, impersonal, conditional. But in the treaties the suzerain addressed his vassal directly: "Thou hast received from me—thou shalt be loyal to me." And this meant that the stipulations likewise were stated in direct address. Hence we have a new construction, hitherto, as far as we can tell, completely unknown in law, but destined to be the favorite and preferred formula in Israel: "Thou shalt," and "Thou shalt not."

In Israel's history the doctrine of the covenant was always fundamental, and it developed in many different ways. Religious infidelity and syncretism, social corruption and immorality, could always be envisaged and excoriated as infidelity to the covenant, which would thereby be voided. The prophets warned that their people were forfeiting all claim on the protection and salvation of Yahweh, by their flouting of the covenant stipulations. In the later prophets, from Hosea on, when the form of the suzerainty treaty had been forgotten, a favorite illustration was taken from a more intimate and domestic covenant, namely, the marriage union. Yahweh became the patient and loving bridegroom, and Israel the shockingly unfaithful wife.

One great advantage of this covenant convention, in its new religious context, was that it so perfectly expressed and safeguarded Yahweh's liberty and authority. If he was the God of Israel it was not by reason of his nature or his origin or a decision of the people. It was uniquely because it had pleased him, who had unlimited possibilities of choice, to select and form this people for himself. The promise "You shall be my people and I will be your God" is at once an announcement and a description of the relationship. It is not explicable or motivated by any quality in the people thus chosen. It depends on the mysterious personality, plans, and preferences of Yahweh, who even in his closest association preserves intact his mystery and his transcendence. The foundation thus laid was permanent, and it belongs to the essence both of Judaism and of Christianity. The God of salvation, the self-revealing God, is demonstrated to be completely independent of the world and the race he has created; but he chooses to extend his care to them, and to work their salvation. His first step in that process is the establishment of covenant, that is, of a new status for men that raises them above whatever natural knowledge and experience they might have of him, and makes them, not just his creatures, not just his servants, but his covenant partners and his sons.

Chapter 4

# The Question of Origins

IN THE PRECEDING PAGES I have tried to show what were the distinctive marks and content of the religion of ancient Israel, not only in the later forms of the postexilic age, or even those of the eighth-century prophets, but at the earliest stage that is accessible to us. Fundamental is the realization of a completely personal God, a super-Person with mind, feelings, and will, who chooses of his own initiative to enter into a personal and moral relationship with them. But along with that fundamental and central belief, almost everything else in Israel's culture was held in common with her more civilized and cultivated neighbors, was in fact borrowed by Israel from them. Israel was, at the time of Moses and for centuries after, a small and relatively insignificant people in the crowded world of the ancient Near East. As descendants of seminomad tribes, only recently initiated into the ways of civilization, the Israelites had to borrow from their neighbors the techniques of which they stood in need. In the plastic arts, in architecture, in government, in the art of war, in material living, Israel was indebted to others, and never showed any great originality. In only one department did she display a genius of her own: that was literature, in the broad sense, in the mastery of language as a medium of expression. And this, as it turned out, was precisely the thing needed for the preservation, propagation, and development of her peculiar religious endowment, the knowledge of her own incomparable God.

That is all the historian can say; he must simply acknowledge the uniqueness of this belief and trace as far as he can its modalities, its development, and the penetrating influence it exerted on every phase of Israelite thinking, and in every crisis of ancient Israel's history.

The theologian, however, must go further; he must declare himself on its validity and its origin. The very basis of the Israelites' faith was their affirmation that this was not a God they had invented but one they had experienced, not a patron they had devised for themselves, but a Being sublime and awe-inspiring, who in an overwhelming display of power had sought them out. They testified to having met him, to having heard his voice, to having known him and been known by him in repeated historical events. He was no illusion, no projection upon the clouds of their own desires or ideals or imaginings; he was tremendously real, and what had been shown to them was only the merest shadow of his unimaginable and fearful greatness, "the whisper of his ways."

In that assertion all believing Jews and all Christians will concur. But this does not excuse the believer from trying to understand better and grasp historically the stages by which Israel's faith developed, and the human aspects and conditioning of this remarkable experience. This process can be examined and discussed scientifically, independently of the ultimate conviction or commitment of the men who examine it.

I propose to discuss next the development in ancient Israel of a fixed doctrine and a coherent belief concerning God's activity in the origins and primeval history of the universe and of mankind. It cannot be too much emphasized that this doctrine was, historically, a secondary development with the Israelites. Their concept of Yahweh, which included from the beginning the essential notes of personality and nonlimitation, developed very greatly in successive problems and challenges. Though much may be implicit, very little is explicitly affirmed about the character of the God of Abraham; and not much more is added in the primitive traditions of Exodus, apart from God's actions in bringing his chosen people out of Egypt and making a covenant with them in the desert. Nothing is affirmed here, for instance, about the relationship to him of other gods, or other nations of the earth; no statement is made about his history—what was he doing before he chose Israel as his people?—or about his activity in nature, or about whether he had anything to do with the creation and origins of things. Nothing is revealed of his future plans, except his general intention to bless and multiply Israel if she is faithful to his covenant. Salvation is the keynote: he is a God who bestows an unhoped-for salvation on this haphazard and insignificant group of very ordinary men. In a word, the Israelites knew Yahweh as savior, as redeemer, before they came to think of him as creator.

Now, in the ideas of the time, gods were the ultimate explanations of things. All the questions that men raise, not immediately answerable by reference to human activity, were explained in terms of divine action. Thus, the origins of the universe, of mankind, and of human society were assigned to a remote past, a mythical age, and pictured as successive stages of the work of various gods. But the very first stipulation of Yahweh's covenant was that Israel should recognize no other gods apart from him. Therefore, by a psychological necessity, he must be for Israel the ultimate explanation of all things. No other God could be acknowledged or thought of. Whatever divine action was to be observed or postulated in the world must by the faithful Israelite be ascribed only to the one God of Israel.

Hence, in modern terms, the development of Israel's theology, in which of course the believer will see at the same time a gradual process of revelation. One crisis after another confronted the faith of Israel with successive challenges: the struggle with the Canaanites, the Philistine danger, the need for the kingship, the schism of the kingdoms, the corruption of the social order, the Assyrian domination, the destruction of Jerusalem, the Exile, the weakness of the postexilic community. Each in its way was a theological problem, and each led Israel, or at least the religious leaders of Israel, to a deeper understanding of God. Their concept of him and his powers became most lofty, just when Israel itself was so weak as to seem on the verge of extinction. This was in the time of the Book of Daniel, in the second century B.C.

But we are concerned now with the first stages of the process, which may have begun even before the time of Moses, among the immediate descendants of Abraham himself, in the light of his exclusive devotion to his personal God. Like all other peoples, Egyptians and Babylonians had their myths, which accounted for the origin of mankind, the origin of the physical universe, the origin of the gods themselves. For the Egyptians, with their conviction of the settled, immutable order of things, the process was pictured as a peaceful one, proceeding step by step according to the designs of the wisest of the gods. In Mesopotamia, where the cosmos was less stable, where human existence was less secure and the elements of natural hazard and human conflict more threatening and frequently destructive, the work of creation was envisaged as achieved and maintained only by a struggle, a violent conflict between the mighty creator-god who aimed at stability and order, and the sullen anarchist powers of chaos which resisted the constitution of an ordered world.

There were many different such myths, of course, but the celebrated *Enuma Elish,* the official canonical version of cosmogony and theogony which was used in the temples in Babylon itself, was the most elaborate and highly developed. It was written on seven tablets and comprises altogether about one thousand lines, though not quite all of it is extant.

*Enuma Elish* begins with the statement of precreation chaos:

> When on high the sky had not been named,
> below the earth had not been called by a name . . .
> no pasture land had been formed,
> no reed marsh was to be seen;
> none of the gods had been brought into being,
> they had not been called by name,
> destinies had not been fixed . . .

All that existed were the sweet water ocean, personified as Apsu, and the salt water ocean, Ti'amat, and their waters were still all mingled together. From them successive generations of gods were produced, including finally the gods of the sky, of the air, and of the earth; and these other divinities, after a time, Ti'amat the symbol of chaos planned to destroy again. The text, as we have it, is the form used in Babylon in the early second millennium B.C., and here the hero who takes up arms against Ti'amat is Marduk, the god of Babylon. In other cities, no doubt, other local gods were given this pre-eminent role. Marduk defeats the she-monster Ti'amat, and out of her carcass he constructs the universe: one half of it is the solid earth; the other half becomes the firmament which holds back the upper waters. He then creates and installs the sun, moon, and stars. Finally, he creates mankind, mixing the blood of a rebellious god, one of Ti'amat's helpers, with clay, for this purpose. Mankind's functions are to serve the gods and supply them with nourishment.

Such in very brief outline is the story of *Enuma Elish*. The characters of the gods here portrayed are no loftier than in other such myths. Some of the deities are positively evil; the hero Marduk acts out of ambition and a wish to surpass and dominate the other gods. No dignity is attributed to men, and certainly no affection is shown for them. A certain amount of wisdom is praised in Marduk and his allies. But morally the story is completely negative. There is nothing to admire, nothing to give thanks for, nothing to imitate, unless it be brute strength. And finally —though Marduk is no doubt capable of maintaining the cosmos he has established—there is no intrinsic assurance that he may not tire, or be overcome, and thus that the powers of chaos may not one day annihilate the world.

Now this myth, or something very similar, must certainly have been familiar to the ancestors of Israel, to the patriarchs and to many generations of their descendants as well. And there are some grounds for saying that when later the Israelites undertook, in opposition to such tales about the gods of Mesopotamia, to establish the sole activity of Yahweh in cosmogony and anthropogony, they presented his work in similar terms, as a battle and a victory over the power of chaos. The references to some such story are found only in poetical contexts, of comparatively late composition; but the resemblances and echoes are unmistakable. There are some half dozen of them, of which I will quote three.

Yahweh is my king from of old,
   worker of salvation in the midst of the earth:
you who divided the sea by your power,
   who crushed the heads of the sea monsters in the waters;
you who shattered the heads of Leviathan,
   who gave him as food to the desert folk;
you who cut open fountain and brook;
   you who dried up unfailing rivers.
To you belong both day and night,
   you who established light and the sun;
you who fixed all the bounds of the earth,
   summer and winter, you have made them. (Ps. 74:12–17.)

Yahweh of hosts, who is like you?
   Your power and your faithfulness are your attendants.
You who rule over the raging of the sea,
   when its waves rise you subdue them;
you who crushed Rahab like a corpse,
   with your strong arm scattered your enemies;
to you belong both sky and earth;
   the world and its contents, you have established them.
                  (Ps. 89:8–11.)

     Awake, awake, put on strength,
       arm of Yahweh!
     Awake, as in the days of old,
       the generations of ancient time.
     Was it not you that mangled Rahab,
       that pierced the sea monster?

> Was it not you that dried up the sea,
>   the waters of the great Deep;
> that made the depths of the sea a pathway
>   for the redeemed to cross by?
>
> (Is. 51:9–10.)

I need not here discuss these passages in detail, or the meanings of Leviathan, Rahab, and the sea monster. I note merely the emphasis on a victorious struggle, a destruction inflicted on adversaries connected with the salt-water ocean, and the relation of this victory with the unchallenged domination of Yahweh over both heaven and earth.

But granted, these are only the debris of an old story, traces of a poetic tradition: we cannot be sure that the tradition itself ever had a fixed, authoritative form, or even that it was recorded in writing. If it was, it never achieved a canonical status; it was not received into the official record of Israel's experience with God—where its logical place would have been at the beginning of Genesis. Very likely, a later and more developed theology shied away from the theme of combat, for the reason that even this gave too much importance to the opponents, too much reality to the powers that resisted Yahweh. Instead, two other creation narratives were selected from the available wealth of tradition, and it is those we now read at the beginning of the Bible.

They are of very different character, and the one generally considered to be of later composition has been appropriately put in first place, as more fundamental. This is the present first chapter of Genesis, describing creation as a work of six days. But Chapters 2 and 3 contain the older story, which already had a long history of oral transmission and development before being fixed in writing, probably about the tenth century B.C.

This older story begins in the traditional style of a creation narrative, conveying the idea of nothingness as a starting point by specifying the things that did not exist:

When Yahweh-God made the earth and the sky,
when as yet no vegetation was on the earth,
when as yet no plants had sprouted—
for Yahweh-God had sent no rain on the earth,
and there were no men to cultivate the soil . . .

But the story does not describe the founding and equipment of the cosmos; its main interest is in the nature of man and his relationship to the Creator. So we hear how the latter took a lump of moist clay, shaped it into a human being, blew in its nostrils, and so gave life to Man. Nor is that all. He plants a garden, an oasis on the dry earth, and installs there this creature made out of clay. In the garden is all that the latter needs for his material sustenance. But one nonmaterial thing is lacking to him—companionship. Yahweh-God forms the animals, as he had Man, out of clay, and parades them before him. But none of them is a fit companion; they are all inferior, subject, Man's servants but not his equals. It is not from clay but from the very person of Man that the desired companion must be formed; and the writer stresses the importance (and perhaps the novelty) of this doctrine of Man and Woman's equality of nature by connecting it with the sexual urge and the institution of marriage: "This is why a man leaves father and mother, to unite himself with a wife; and the two of them make up a single being."

If the story stopped there, one would already have plenty of material for drawing a contrast with Babylonian conceptions of human nature and the work of the gods. But there is far more. The Yahwist, great genius that he was, had unequaled insight into human psychology, as well as into the implications of the already traditional faith of Israel. There was obviously a huge gap, not just of time but of status, between that idyllic, perfectly harmonious existence, and human life as he knew it and as we know it today. He undertakes to account for this difference, and he locates it fundamentally, not in altered external circumstances, but, religiously, in man's altered relationship to God.

In the marvelous garden are two special trees, whose fruit denotes qualities and powers belonging properly to divinity: the tree of life, symbol of immortality, and the tree of knowledge of good and evil, symbol of dominion over good and evil—as we should say, of the power of establishing moral values, of deciding right and wrong. The latter alone is forbidden to Man's use. We may note how the Yahwist instinctively portrays Yahweh as a covenant God; just as the stipulations of the Sinai covenant were a series mainly of prohibitions stated in personal terms, so he expresses the divine prescription in the same form: "Thou shalt not eat the fruit of the tree of knowledge." There is, then, an implied covenant relationship between the Creator-God and mankind.

But the covenant is broken by Man—or rather, first, by the Woman. The Snake appears, a being of Yahweh-God's creation (as the author is careful to specify; he will run no risk of dualism by making the Snake independent of Yahweh), yet mysteriously hostile to him, envious of his favorite creatures, and gifted with strange knowledge and great cunning. Misled by him, invited to make themselves like gods, Woman and Man transgress the command, break the covenant, and find that instead of rising to the level of independent gods they have fallen even from what they were. On the original unity and harmony of their existence, their sin has a divisive effect: it alienates them from their Creator, it sets them at odds with one another, it destroys the internal harmony and order of their own consciences. Even before sentence is passed, Man and Woman condemn themselves to exile, by hiding in their shame from the sight of their benefactor.

This inadequate sketch of a great and famous passage will illustrate two points. The first is its similarity in style and imagery with many a story of creation in other literatures. The language, the conventions, the symbols belong to a fixed and familiar genre, which owes most to the myths of Babylonia. In no other terms could a cosmogony or anthropogony be acceptable or comprehensible to the mentality of early Israel. It had to tell a story; it had to embody its teaching in such images as a wonderful garden, a talking snake, a magic tree.

Secondly, no ancient literature offers any parallel to the profundity, the penetration, with which psychological and theological truths are here so plastically expressed. They all depend on the central figure of the story, who is neither the Man nor the Woman, still less the Snake, but the Creator-God himself. No explanation is attempted of his origin; he is there, given, existent; the question is only to explain the origin of his creatures. He does not need them; but he creates them and then lavishes on them his benefactions. The only return he expects from them, and the only one they can give him, is their personal loyalty, their acknowledgment of the truth that they are his. When they deplorably fail in this acknowledgment, and attempt to dispense with him—when they break the covenant of loyalty and gratitude—their punishment is less than they deserve, is tempered with indulgent mercy, and does not completely separate them from him.

This ethical emphasis, the moral imperative inseparable from the covenant doctrine, is perhaps the outstanding difference in tone and atmosphere between this account and Babylonian myths. This God has the knowledge of good and evil, which means that he decides what they are. Acceptance of his standards is the central obligation for the humanity that is dependent on him. A deep mystery is left about his own internal plans; but there is perfect clarity in the demands he makes of men.

We may notice also the universalism proper to a story about creation. Yahweh had deigned to become the God of Israel and to take Israel as his people. But here, before Israel even existed, long before Abraham was born, at the origin of humanity itself he is shown as present and acting with his usual power, wisdom, and love. Only, he is the God, the only God, of humanity as such. All other divinities are excluded. And so is Israel excluded. The Israelites were well aware that they had arrived late in history. *Enuma Elish* had pictured the climax of Marduk's work as the building of the city of Babylon and the founding of his temple in it. But the Israelite author is not even tempted to bring Israel into his story so early. He knows that this would not be the truth; and anyway he is intent on glorifying his God—not his people, and not the human race.

We may now consider the more formal and scientific treatise, the cosmogony properly so-called, which is preserved as the opening chapter of Genesis. The literary form of this piece is something of a puzzle: it is not a prophetic oracle, not a chronicle, not a psalm, not a piece of wisdom writing. It is in prose, but prose that has a marked and majestic rhythm, with deliberate and solemn repetitions. The best identification is to call it a liturgical text, elaborately composed for public recitation on a feast day, which almost surely was the new year's feast. In Babylon, *Enuma Elish* was twice publicly recited in the eleven-day celebration that marked the new year's festival; and if this was the Israelite equivalent and counterpart, then we see that in that respect as in several others it had a deliberately polemical intention: it aimed at contradicting and displacing the Babylonian doctrine of creation.

The structure of the piece is simple, but carefully worked out. After an introduction, which gives the usual description of the nothingness from which creation must start, there follows the famous hexaemeron, the work of six days. But the stages of the work overlap: there are eight "works," eight creative acts, and to fit them into the six-day framework the third and sixth days must contain two works each. It is likely that this overlapping is a trace of the long literary history that lies behind the present text; the division of creation into eight works must have come first and later have been compressed into the six-day scheme, for the sake of teaching the sanctity of the sabbath. Other such traces may be found in a double statement of the divine productivity. First it is presented as a command, then as an action: that is, "God said, 'Let there be a firmament,' " and then, "God made the firmament."

At all events, the final form in which the text is fixed—dating very likely from the sixth or fifth century B.C. and the work of Jewish exiles in Babylonia—is a highly skillful and unified composition. It is really not correct to think of this account as naive or even unscientific. It is a very learned document, elaborately composed and polished with the purpose of setting forth an important doctrine, and it makes careful and conscientious use of the scientific concepts of the time. For example, the threefold botanical division of grass, plants, and seed-bearing trees is that adopted in the Babylonian lexicons. Similarly, the threefold classification of land creatures, as wild animals, domestic animals, and creeping things, is borrowed from contemporary science. On a larger scale, the cosmography, the concepts of the sky as a solid hemispherical vault holding back the upper waters, of the waters below the earth, of the heavenly bodies as traversing the firmament —these define the world picture familiar at least to all educated people of the time. This scientific exactness— for so it deserves to be called—is part of the plan: the doctrine the authors are concerned to convey aims at completeness. Everything is the work of Yahweh, and no corner of the universe is left unclaimed, for the possible operation of other gods. In particular, emphasis is laid on the devaluation of sun, moon, and stars. To the Babylonians, these were important divinities in their own right. Israel's theologians disdain even to use the names of sun and moon. They call them the greater light and the lesser light, and they present them as created to be calendar markers for the liturgical benefit of Israel: "Let them serve as signs, and for the fixing of seasons, days, and years."

But those are merely some of the details. The authors' main concern is their doctrine about the Creator-God; and here we find a more complete and developed theology than in any passage we have considered so far. Here is a mature theological doctrine, conscious of itself and confident in its technique. The opening sentence establishes the tone: "In the beginning God created the sky and the earth." That is best taken as a summary of all that follows, a sort of title. Then there comes the starting point: "The earth was chaotic and void, and darkness lay over the surface of the deep." This is as close as Semitic expression could come to metaphysical nothingness: chaos, darkness, and the deep are the very symbols of nothingness, of non-existence, and on them or at least against that background the divine activity is exerted. From the nothingness of darkness is produced the primary creature, light. "God said, 'Let light be'; and light came to be." The phrase has been rightly admired as a triumph of poetic imagination; but the priestly writers were not greatly gifted as poets, and to them it came, one might say, almost as a philosophical consequence. If darkness was the symbol for nonbeing, then the primary effect of creation must be light.

Again we observe the refusal to develop any theogony. The God of Israel is the only God; he has no pantheon around him, no female consort beside him (classical Hebrew has not even recorded any word for "goddess"). For his being there, no explanation is required and none is possible. He is simply present, living, before the beginning. But his ethical character is prominent as ever; in the first stages, before man appears, there is repeated emphasis on the Creator's concern that things be good. Goodness is what he plans and intends, and each work is checked to ensure that it measures up to his standard.

Majestically the sequence proceeds. There is first the series of divisions—light from darkness, upper waters from lower, dry land from sea. With the clothing of the earth in vegetation, the preparation of the areas of the cosmos is complete. The second series of works, in the fourth, fifth, and sixth days, provides the mobile occupants of the established areas: the lights in the sky, the fish and birds in sea and air, the living creatures on the earth, and finally, mankind. And here, so far as reason need be given for this outpouring of creative power, it appears to be mainly for the benefit of man. God's only profit otherwise is his satisfaction in the goodness of creation. But man is to be gifted with dominion and power over all other creatures. Even his creation is presented very differently: there is a preliminary deliberation, a threefold enunciation of man's origin, and special provision for his sustenance. Noteworthy is the doctrine of his creation in the image and likeness of the Creator.

> God created man:
> In the image of God he created them;
> Male and female, he created them both.

There follows the blessing of fertility. This is thought of as separate from the gift of life; it needs separate actuation, so to speak. Again, the polemical purpose is clear. If any Israelites, acknowledging Yahweh as their God, were tempted nevertheless to apply to the Babylonian or Canaanite gods of fertility for the blessing of offspring, they should learn here that the mystery and power of procreation come likewise from Israel's God, and that he introduced it into his original blessing of all mankind.

There is one prominent difference between the older story of the Garden of Eden and this cosmology: no moral element is here introduced, other than the sheer goodness of the Creator-God. There is no prohibition laid on mankind, no account of a rebellion and fall. The latter is not positively excluded; but the purpose of the priestly writers was to develop and stress the divine creative providence, action, and conservation. They were not concerned with human reactions, even human history as such —only with establishing their sublime doctrine concerning the Creator himself. In the priestly tradition, as it can be discerned in the first chapters of Genesis, there is no reference to human infidelity and sin, until it becomes necessary to explain the catastrophe of the Flood.

Such are the main presentations in Israelite literature of the origins of the world and the human race. They owe it to their theological content and teaching that they are so infinitely superior to other contemporary cosmogonies, that they can speak to men of later ages, and quite different cultures, with unfailing power and effect. The literary conventions here followed, the usage of symbol and imagery, the world picture which is presupposed—all these are simply a medium of expression, conditioned by the authors' time and place. Naturally, they do not use the conventions and images that are familiar to us. But, rightly understood, their symbolism is no handicap to our penetrating and profiting by their teaching. The truths they affirm are part of the patrimony of Christian and Jew alike. It would be very shortsighted even for the unbeliever, repelled by this antique formulation, to dismiss the narratives as outworn and abandoned myths. No better explanations, certainly, have yet been put forward in theistic terms than these devised by the faith and reflection of ancient Israel.

Chapter 5

# The Problem of Myth and History

THE TITLE OF this chapter indicates a vast and ambitious subject, and it is well to specify from the outset that I intend to treat of only one special case of it, namely, the form that the problem assumes within the context of this discussion of theological significance of the Old Testament. As we have seen in considering the creation narratives, there undoubtedly are myths contained in the Old Testament, not of course polytheistic myths but narratives invented to explain the ultimate reasons of things, and to express the mythmaker's faith in a particular divine activity. Once such an explanation steps outside the familiar world of everyday life, and appeals to the work of God done outside the time and space that we know, there is no other recourse but the language of myth to convey the important truths that men need to apprehend. We have seen how much of the vocabulary of ordinary mythmaking, how much of its imagery and symbols, especially in the story of the Garden of Eden, is taken from the common stock of Near Eastern mythology.

But the problem of the relationship of myth to history, of the amount of truth expressed by each, and of the manner in which it is expressed, arises in the Old Testament not so much because of the presence there of myth as because of the presence there of so much history. The religion of ancient Israel differed conspicuously from the other religions of that time and area in claiming to be founded on historical events. This claim it has in common with Christianity. Broadly speaking, Israel's credo is presented as a revelation from God that occurred at specific times in specific places to identifiable men. And from those men to the contemporary generation there is an unbroken line

69

of transmission, partly oral, partly written, which perpetu-
ates their testimony to this experience of the divine, this
message from on high. As we know, the events recorded
in the New Testament occurred in a well-known historical
period, and within a definite and small geographical area.
Galilee, central Palestine, Judea and Jerusalem make up
the scene; and the time is specified in the Church's creed
as "under Pontius Pilate," Roman procurator of the southern part of the province of Syria in the years 26 to 36 A.D.
Similarly with the events of the Old Testament which fell
within the experience of Israel itself: the foundation of the
faith of the Israelites lies in their memory of their onetime
residence, and oppression, in Egypt, and of their being
brought out thence and granted a covenant by a distinctive
and unique God, to whom ever since they have been inescapably bound. And this also, though they could not
pin it down so closely in time and space as the Evangelists
do their history, is a series of events experienced by flesh
and blood people, with whom they knew themselves to be
akin—with whom, in fact, collectively, they simply identified themselves.

Now against this down-to-earth realism of the Hebrew
and Christian traditions, the mythologies properly so called
of pagan religions, in Egypt, Mesopotamia, or ancient
Greece, have a totally unreal air and character. No question of verification or tradition arises. When we hear how
Osiris was slain, how Marduk became king of the gods, or
how the Titans revolted against Cronos, the story belongs
to another world than ours; and I mean to another world
than that of ordinary human experience, whether of our
time or the time of the men in Egypt or Mesopotamia or
Greece who developed these mythologies. Such narratives
are properly mythological statements, to be either accepted
or rejected as significant or otherwise—in either case it is
useless and meaningless to inquire, for example, how such
a story became known. It is simply there, it is narrated
and listened to, and it tells of some mysterious reality
which is of importance to the teller and the hearers. But

even to them it is not history in the sense of a transmitted record of human experience. "It seems most unlikely that the Assyrians would have regarded the story of Ishtar's descent to the underworld as the same type of story which might be told of Sennacherib's victorious campaign in Western Asia."*

Because of this unreal and unverifiable character of the highly elaborate mythologies of these great civilizations, myth as such has been defined and understood as a purely imaginary story, "a story about gods," devoid of truth and significance. But thus to brush it aside is overhasty. Modern ethnologists, anthropologists, and historians of culture habitually devote close attention to mythology, and they find not only that it was of fundamental importance to the people who created and narrated it, but that it has much to tell us about their psychology and social and religious outlook, and about human psychology and behavior in general. Myth is always an attempt to express, and thereby to make comprehensible, some truth about the world and man's existence in it, a truth inaccessible and unknown in itself, but capable of being expressed in and by symbols. It is not of the essence of myth that it should be polytheist, telling stories about gods and goddesses. What is essential is that it should attempt to formulate transcendental reality, to reach something behind the flux of phenomena that envelops human existence, to pin down an absolute in which the human mind can rest with some feeling of security. The mythical event is always presented as taking place in the past, but there is also felt in it some contemporary relevance. Often the narrative is etiological, giving an explanation why things are as they are. Even when it is not thus explanatory, it nevertheless is somehow effective for the hearers.

This brings us to the connection between myth and ritual. It is an unwarranted exaggeration to maintain that all myth is the libretto, so to call it, of some ritual; there are

* John L. McKenzie, in "Myth and the Old Testament," *Catholic Biblical Quarterly*, 21 (1959), p. 268.

far too many exceptions to allow that to be a valid rule. But it is true that in the cities and sanctuaries and temples of the ancient world the myths in many cases were dramatically acted out, with the text recited as interpretative accompaniment. Two of the celebrated examples are the mourning for Adonis, annually performed by women in Syria and elsewhere, and the Babylonian new year's festival, at which Marduk's triumph over the powers of chaos, and his establishment of an ordered and hierarchical world, were re-enacted and made operative for another year. In such instances there is no mistaking the power that is attached to the myth. The salvation or creation or vivification that it narrates and symbolizes is actuated anew, becomes contemporary and effective in this re-presentation.

Now we come to the other point of comparison, history. Here one must allow for the vulgar prejudice that history is a kind of objective existent, independent of the human mind, to which the human verbal presentation can come, and ideally should come, indefinitely close. It is not, I hope, necessary to labor the point that this mistakes the nature of history, and its relation to the raw material of human acts and natural phenomena. From the quasi-infinite abundance of actions and things, only a tiny fraction of which is recorded in documents or survives in human memories, history is constructed by selection and arrangement. It is a work of the human spirit, perceiving significance, sequence, and causality in occurrences that need both selection and interpretation in order to become meaningful. This significance—which is perfectly objective and real—may be conceived already in the mind of the participants, and at all events is grasped by that of the historian. A fairly modern example might be Napoleon's Russian campaign, which is treated in history books as an event significant and comprehensible by itself, with a beginning, middle, and end. The raw material in reality is a certain period of time and an infinity of experiences in the lives of many thousands of people. By a very limited selection from that material the historian can disclose the unity and effects of a certain whole. (It can be done and has been done with equal effectiveness by a novelist—Tolstoy—and by a poet—Thomas Hardy.)

And this is where history and myth meet one another. The story of the Napoleonic campaign in Russia—the defeat, and the famous retreat from Moscow—became a myth in the modern sense, and one that showed itself strangely effective in World War II. According to this generalized concept, a myth is a narrative about the past which is meaningful and operative in the present. It symbolizes and constitutes, for those who listen to it or narrate it or act it out, a lived experience of the significant past reality.

Granted, there does remain an important difference in the reality of the characters who act in ancient and modern myths—whether they were originally flesh and blood figures or purely imagined ones. But even so, the flesh and blood figures in their original concrete reality do not suffice to influence later generations. They must be mythicized, understood and presented as meaningful and relevant; a good deal of imagination plays around such figures as Christopher Columbus or George Washington, and what the average man carries in his mind and heart about either of them has the character more of mythical statement than of mere historical accuracy. Historical pageants, in modern times, are the secularized equivalents of the rituals of ancient Babylon. By dramatizing, say, the arrival of the Pilgrim Fathers at Plymouth Rock, or, on the local level, the founding of some particular settlement or city, modern Americans renew contact with the sources of their history, affirm their unity with the pioneers, perform a ritual that reinforces patriotism and civic pride. And, one must repeat, as regards the efficacy of such a ritual, the degree of strict historicity in the incident recreated is irrelevant and does not affect its mythic value. George Washington may never have cut down a cherry tree; but that need not detract from the mythic effectiveness of the story. It is the meaning seen in it by contemporaries that is of importance.

I have no wish to confuse mythology and history; I wish

only to show that they are not complete opposites, and that each has in it something of the other. History is not quite as historical, and myth is not quite as mythical, as we tend to think.

Now having stressed so much the historical character of Israel's self-consciousness, the historical form her national memory took, I must qualify that by showing the large part played in it by myth in this modern sense of the word. For examples, there are David and Solomon. In spite of, or perhaps aided by, the large quantity of genuine historical traditions about these two men, each of them, as a figure remembered in tradition, gathered mythical qualities and significance in the minds of later generations. Concerning David, much contemporary eyewitness material has been preserved, particularly in the superb piece of historical prose that makes up 2 Samuel 9 to 20, and 1 Kings 1 and 2. There we see him as in a series of candid snapshots, a fascinating character, a mixture of saintliness and cunning, of generosity and self-interest, of nobility and treachery. But that realistic and detailed portrait yielded in later books, such as Chronicles, to a simplified and idealized conception which glorified David simply as the divinely approved king, graced by a special family covenant with God, the very pledge and exemplar of the human instrument by which Yahweh's final salvation would be effected. It has been said that the Chronicler makes David into a royal sacristan—a slight exaggeration perhaps, but certainly his is not a very recognizable picture of David as he must have been in life. Yet it is a perfectly legitimate and valid statement of what David had become after death, of his significance to postexilic Israel. Similarly with Solomon, a colder and less fascinating character: he is mythicized as the paragon of wisdom, the successful and peaceful ruler, the model of human prosperity, showing how gloriously it could fare with a man who enjoyed the fullness of Yahweh's blessing.

Similar remarks could be made concerning the figures of Moses, Joshua, Samuel, and other great heroes of Israel's history. It is pointless to accuse Israel's later historiographers of distortion, anachronism, or the arbitary re-writing of history. What they were doing was perfectly valid. They were simply expressing the meaning of these great figures of the past to their own contemporaries; and they must be judged on the basis of their own aims and intentions—not by how they matched up to the ideals of nineteenth-century Western historiography.

But there is another section of the Israelites' literary tradition where we come much closer to mythology properly so called. This is the section dealing with the period before their own existence, for which they had no tradition of their own. In the nature of things they were here dependent on earlier material; and such material they could draw only from the corpus of myths and folklore gathered and transmitted by other peoples.

Something of this we have seen in their creation narratives; and the same motivation, naturally, was at work. Their own history was brief; but the history of Yahweh, their God, was something quite different. They had not called him into existence. He had always been there; and just from what one might call the apologetic point of view, it was important that they should express and maintain their faith that he was incomparably superior to all the gods of the Gentiles—not merely in their own experience of him, but before that, from all time.

Therefore they had their stories of creation, in which the imagery and conventions were borrowed naturally from the existing genre, and the specific differences came merely from the peculiar character of the God shown at work. But the mythmaking had to be carried further. An immense interval of time separated the era of creation from the call of Abraham, and that gap too had to be filled with some version of Yahweh's activity.

The material they found, and adapted, to express this activity is roughly what is contained in Chapters 4 to 11 of the Book of Genesis. It spans the interval referred to above. To constitute it, a selection was made from a large body of material relating to prehistoric, mythical time. Thus, they constructed a genealogy out of twenty traditional names, joining to them numbers of years which would indicate the immense span of time covered, and its remoteness from the contemporary world. Then they pieced out this genealogy with a handful of stories, each of which could be and was adapted to express the sole presence and government, in this prehistoric world, of their just and holy God. In particular, they made much of the outstanding item of Near Eastern prehistory, which was the story of the great Flood. Of this story we also have several Mesopotamian versions; and we can trace with fair assurance the amount and type of revision the story underwent, in being transferred into the corpus of Israelite doctrinal narratives.

The Babylonian version shows the usual theme of a conflict between the gods. The plan to annihilate the human race is nothing more than a caprice of one of the gods, who is irritated at the commotion caused by the race of men. One man and his family are saved by the favoritism shown them by another deity. In other details, there are many interesting resemblances to the version in Genesis, particularly the mention of releasing birds on shipboard to see if there is dry land nearby—a point that guarantees the eastern provenance of the Israelite tradition, since this device was unknown in Mediterranean navigation but did belong to the Indian Ocean, and therefore was practiced by mariners sailing out of the Persian Gulf.

The Babylonian myth (its most complete form has been transmitted to us as a secondary insertion in the Epic of Gilgamesh) was naturally related to the fortunes of its hearers; the lesson was the future survival of the race, which had once thus been threatened with utter destruction and had nevertheless survived. That is, the story contained an element of reassurance in the face of threatening cataclysms of nature. This too has been preserved in the Israelite account, where the story ends with the guarantee that the Flood will not return—of which the rainbow is made the symbol—and with a solemn divine oracle promising the continued operation of the cosmos:

> As long as the earth lasts,
> seedtime and harvest, cold and heat,
> summer and winter, day and night,
> shall never cease. (Gen. 8:22)

But the main difference, as usual, is produced by the character of Yahweh. It was unthinkable that he should act merely by caprice, unreasonably and unethically. This tremendous visitation, which was almost a reversal of his creation and a reduction of all things to the primeval state of chaos, must have a moral motivation. And that the Israelite instinctively found in the moral corruption of the race of men. It is their chronic rebelliousness, their ungrateful repudiation of the authority of their Lord and Benefactor, the flouting of his sanctity and justice, which almost compel the just God to punish them. The Yahwist tradition, with its deep theological insight expressed in naively anthropomorphic terms, puts this with bold and impressive realism:

When Yahweh saw how great was the wickedness of man upon the earth, and that all the desires of his heart were bent only upon evil all day long, Yahweh regretted that he had ever made man on the earth, and he was grieved to the heart. (Gen. 6:5–6.)

This image of the grief-stricken God is certainly daring, and later generations increasingly shrank from such naive expressions, for fear of seeming to make Yahweh too human. But they did not expunge it from the old story, and for that we should be grateful. For Israel, the God who sends the Flood is a God touched to the heart with sorrow, who, unwillingly compelled by his own justice, cannot allow sin to go unpunished. This is the negative side of his rejoicing in goodness, as we saw it portrayed in one of the creation narratives.

Merely from this detail, we have enough to understand the biblical use of mythology, and the amount of history that is included in it. The story of the Flood was the common property of the Near East in the second millennium; probably everybody knew the story in some form or other, just as everybody believed in the solidity of the firmament and the presence of waters above the firmament. Whether the tradition had some historic origin in one particularly calamitous inundation in Mesopotamia, we cannot now tell, and the question has little interest. In the versions that we know, the account is not a historical narrative but a mythological one. That is, it is not really a story about a "natural phenomenon"; it is a story about the gods and how they sent a "divine" Flood.

Now, the Israelites could not pretend ignorance of this already familiar and widespread tradition. But they could do something about it, by retelling it so as to demonstrate the real forces at work. What they make of it has been indicated: it becomes in their hands an intensely impressive and pathetic portrayal of the historic reality of human sin and of the reaction of Yahweh to it. And herein lies their teaching, and the historical affirmation they wish to make by means of this mythological form. Humanity has always tended to rebelliousness, to ingratitude and self-assertion. And its creator has always shown himself a vindicator of justice, a punisher of iniquity, and yet at the same time faithful in preserving those who are faithful to him, and indulgent and merciful to the race as a whole.*

On a smaller scale, the same technique is seen at work in the enigmatic fragment of a story placed by the Yahwist as an introduction to his narrative of the Flood:

When mankind began to grow numerous on the earth, and daughters were born to them, the sons of Elohim saw that the

---

* If this last remark sounds strange, in view of the almost total destruction of humanity in the Flood story, it is nevertheless justified from the narrators' point of view. To them the human race is the existing postdiluvian people, descendants of the righteous Noah. The corrupt antediluvians are an incarnation of evil, and their removal is not only a vindication of God's goodness in itself but also a merciful deliverance for the survivors. It is parallel to the defeat and subjection of the powers of chaos, the necessary preliminary to the establishment of an ordered and good universe.

daughters of men were attractive. So they married those whom they liked best. Then Yahweh said, "My spirit shall not remain in mankind forever, as they are flesh. Their lifetime shall be one hundred and twenty years." In those days there were giants on the earth, born to the sons of Elohim when they had intercourse with the daughters of men . . . (Gen. 6:1–4.)

Elohim may mean "gods" or "God"; and sons of Elohim would normally mean "divinities." Perhaps "heavenly beings" comes closest to the idea. It is hard to be sure of the lesson of the original story. But we can see the use the Yahwist makes of it. The intervention of these "heavenly" or at least superhuman beings becomes a parallel to the introduction of the Snake in Genesis 3. For the second time, the corruption of humanity is attributed to extraterrestrial powers, and they exert this fatal influence through the female sex. Just enough of the story is quoted to convey this idea, which leads up to the state of extreme moral corruption needed to introduce and justify the Flood.

Another example might be the story of the tower of Babel, or rather Babylon, in Chapter 11. (Everywhere else *bab'el* is correctly translated "Babylon." Why should an exception be made here?) This obviously presupposes an etiological myth which accounted for the variety of languages among peoples and linked it up with the story of an unfinished temple tower, one of the so-called *ziggurats* in the city of Babylon. But this comparatively trivial bit of mythmaking is completely transformed when the Israelite theologian takes it up as a vehicle of his doctrine and introduces into it the majestic figure of his God. It becomes another parallel to the story of the Garden of Eden, another statement of the now familiar theme of human ambition asserting itself, of man's insubordinate pride in seeking to become like God. It shows the God of Israel acting with his usual serene majesty, and after due inquiry and judgment inflicting the just yet merciful penalty. At the same time, in its present context the story is skillfully located so as to form a background to the great positive act of salvation which is the call of Abraham. The story of the tower of Babylon closes the series of pre-Israelite and therefore prehistoric narratives with the despairing picture of a humanity scattered, disunited, homeless, and above all alienated from its Creator and Lord. The divisive effect of sin is shown again here, and even more dramatically. The diversity of languages is here not merely a sociological fact or a normal ethnological development. It is pictured not as a consequence but as a cause of the diffusion and dispersal of the race. It has become a symbol of mutual incomprehension between peoples, producing hostility and conflict. The race is not only separated from its God but fragmentary and divided in itself. Against that dark background of mankind's desperate need for rescue and salvation is set in the following chapter the divine act by which one man is summoned, to become eventually the father of a whole people of God—more than that, to become eventually a channel of blessing and salvation to all the families of the earth.

One may say then that, where the authors of Israel had historical traditions to draw on, they used them conscientiously and faithfully. It was not of course secular or materialist history they were writing. It was religious history, an account of the deeds of their God as witnessed by them, which they were in duty bound to pass on to the generations to come. The significance they saw in the events, and (more or less crudely and naively) expressed in their accounts of them, was a significance perceived by the eye of faith, though they could also have claimed it was confirmed by experience. But in any case, event and interpretation were one and inseparable. The Israelite historians were not interested, as we are, in trying to separate the divine action perceived by faith from "what really happened." For them, what really happened was what God did, and the material phenomena on the level of sense perception could be freely heightened and colored in their accounts, the better to express the reality that lay behind them.

But when they had no history and traditions of their own, namely, for the period preceding the call of Abraham, then they were of necessity driven to take their materials where they could find them, and that meant only in the tradition and mythology that had originated among other peoples. This was a necessity, unless they were willing to give the impression, and even admit to themselves, that their covenant God, whom they believed to surpass incomparably all the so-called gods of the Gentiles, had had no effective existence, had exercised no control over mankind and the universe, before the time of Abraham. But that was unthinkable. Hence their adoption and adaptation of older traditional materials, which I have attempted to describe. I must insist again that they knew what they were doing. They could not investigate or check, and hence could not guarantee, the historicity of the stories, as we now understand historicity. But the doctrine which Israel attached to them and expressed through them, that is historical: namely, that the God who called Abraham was and had always been sole Lord and Ruler in heaven and on earth; that mankind as such had always had moral responsibility for its behavior; that men by and large had been sinful, and had often impiously asserted their claims and ambitions against the sanctity of the Creator; that, finally, God had sanctioned his laws by penalties and judgments, yet had always displayed the character of mercy and goodness which Israel had come to know—in short, he had always been a God of salvation, in whom men could safely place their entire confidence and trust.

Chapter 6

## The Search for Wisdom

THE TWENTY-EIGHTH CHAPTER of the Book of Job contains an independent poem whose refrain is "Where can Wisdom be found? And where is the place of understanding?" With haunting imagery, the poem goes on to deny wisdom's accessibility to all things created: "Man knows not the way of it, nor is it found in the land of the living. The abyss says, 'It is not in me'; the sea says, 'I have it not.' " For wisdom is uniquely a divine possession: "Only God understands its way, and he knows its location."

We have here described one of the great searches of ancient man—and, one might add, of modern man as well. Where can wisdom be found? In what does it consist? The pessimistic conclusion of the ancient poet declares the quest to be a hopeless one from the start, unless indeed—for he leaves this possibility open—God should choose freely to communicate to man what the latter by his own efforts is unable ever to discover. But this refers to divine wisdom. The ancient world was not generally so pessimistic about the acquiring of *some* wisdom. The wisdom teaching and the sapiential literature of the ancient Near East comprise quite copious collections of material, even in the fragmentary state in which they have been transmitted to us. I shall try to trace here the relationship of this study, this investigation of wisdom, to the distinctive religious outlook of Israel: in particular, how it reacted with, and was eventually assimilated by, the specific belief concerning the nature and activity of Israel's covenant God.

The concept of wisdom here in question is a wide one, more all-embracing than anything we are familiar with today. It might be said to include, in very primitive forms, what we would now call philosophy, in all its branches, and the social sciences in particular; originally it could even refer to social and technical skills of any kind. In fact, this is probably its root meaning; the Hebrew word *hokmah* meant primarily the technical know-how of the agriculturist or the artisan or the skilled warrior; or more vaguely, the skill and expertise of the professional counselor, the wise man who was never at a loss in ticklish situations. We see wisdom then, in its very broadest acceptance, as equivalent to human culture, to the slow and painfully won acquisitions that marked man's gradual but increasingly swift ascent from a state of brutish savagery to the level of the first great civilizations which history discloses to us.

Even peoples whom we would consider "primitive" have their folk wisdom, as it is called; folk wisdom is not only the possession of inherited skills and techniques, of hunting, of erecting shelters, of preparing food, of weaving, pottery making, and the like, but verbal formulations and descriptions of these and similar procedures. Further, it goes a step beyond the verbalizing of technical, material skills, to formulate more elusive principles of human behavior, norms of social adjustment and methods of influencing or dominating one's personal environment. These are expressed particularly in the form of proverbs, wise sayings or maxims concerning human behavior, whether observed or prescribed. There is hardly any human society so far discovered which is without some such corpus of traditional wisdom, embodied in curt and memorable sentences.

But the sophisticated wisdom we are now considering as a subject of literature has developed a long way from this naive and popular proverb making. Just as certain men were outstanding warriors or hunters or sorcerers, so there were individuals particularly gifted in discernment, in prudence, in giving counsel in human affairs. These are the sages, the wise men, whose pre-eminence is due partly to the accumulated experience of age and tradition, partly to an innate gift which was naturally seen as a precious endowment from the gods.

In relation to our study of the ancient Near East, we may consider wisdom first in Egypt. There we have, from as far back as the late third millennium B.C., collections of wisdom instructions, designed to pass on to future generations the accumulated insight and experimental judgments of the past. These naturally are recorded in writing; and so we find from the beginning the association that marked the history of this Near Eastern sapiential tradition. It is constantly associated with—more than that, it is the proper possession of—the guild or profession of the scribes.

There is an apparent exception, in that a favorite form of the earliest Egyptian wisdom material is that of instructions passed on to his successor by a high official, a vizier, or even the Pharaoh himself. These are probably literary fictions; but even if the Pharaoh and various high officials were the authors, their instructions were recorded, were studied and transmitted, by Egyptian scribes. And these scribes, who were necessarily a small and select group, formed a very important section of the governing class in Egypt. Whether attached to temples or to the royal administration, they were key men, indispensable agents in the elaborate bureaucracy of this highly centralized state. Along with the work of day-to-day administration, they had their own professional interests, and prominent among these were the study and transmission, and even the composition, of works of wisdom. The lengthy training of apprentices to carry on the tradition was naturally of great importance, and one of the means of boosting the prestige of this arduous profession was to stress that only the scribe could be truly wise. Some of their instructions, it is true, hardly aim at more than forming the perfect civil servant. The scribe who is trustworthy, discreet, loyal to his master, honest and incorruptible will rise to the highest positions in Egypt, even to that of vizier. But the motivation is not limited to enlightened self-interest. Virtues such as truth, modesty, philanthropy, and reverence for the gods are presented as absolute goods, objects to be striven for by the young man who wishes not only to be successful in life, but also to measure up to a certain ethical ideal of virtue and right conduct.

Passing now to the other great civilization of the Bronze Age, in Mesopotamia, we find a roughly parallel development. There also a wisdom tradition grew up which produced an elaborate and sophisticated literature. There also a very difficult system of writing, requiring years of training and practice for its mastery, limited literacy to a comparatively small group of men, who similarly claimed a quasi-monopoly of professional wisdom. The Mesopotamian scribes made collections of proverbs and of fables, wrote parables, composed dialogues between imaginary characters, and of course put together manuals of instruction in etiquette and protocol, in the management of men, and in the means of harmonious adjustment to society and to the gods. This development was well launched by the pre-Semitic settlers of southern Babylonia, the Sumerians, who were the inventors of cuneiform writing; but it was carried on and expanded by their Babylonian successors.

The Egyptian sages had as their environment the peculiarly stable way of life, as regards both its physical setting and the fixity of its social structure, which was mentioned earlier. Only rare periods of political turmoil and disorganization confronted them with problems concerning the goodness of life and the validity of the divine control of the cosmos. The Babylonians, on the other hand, living in an environment physically more hazardous and threatening, and politically more unstable, even revolutionary, were constantly preoccupied with the human situation, and the consequent theological problem of man's position relative to the gods. This probably is why the Babylonian sages pushed their speculation a stage beyond that of the Egyptians, to include their great debates and questionings on the justice of the gods, on the ultimate value of human existence, and on possible means of securing the salvation and fulfillment which all men desire.

Beginning with Sumerian literature, there are extant five or six full-scale discussions of the problem of human existence, which found its crowning treatment in the Hebrew Book of Job.

The Israelites, emerging from the desert as a league of barbarous seminomadic tribes, rapidly implanted themselves in the fertile land of Canaan, and almost as rapidly shed their barbarism and acquired the civilization of the time. The crucial step perhaps was their adoption, in the eleventh century B.C., of hereditary kingship as their political system; for this quickly brought other radical cultural changes along with it. A capital city was chosen, a temple was built, a royal court was established, and a central fiscal administration was organized. The three last steps were taken by Solomon, and it is no accident, but solid historical tradition, that associates his name preeminently with the introduction of wisdom to Israel—the introduction, that is, of professional wisdom as distinct from folk wisdom, of which Israel like other nations already had its own tradition. For his centralized government, for collection of taxes, keeping of records, instructions to officials, and diplomatic correspondence, Solomon had need of a professional corps of scribes, on the model of the Pharaonic bureaucracy. It may well be that he sought help from Egyptian officials in the organizing of his chancellery; in any case, we see the scribal guild quickly established in Jerusalem, and in addition to its administrative functions exercising from the start its patronage of sapiential literature, its training of the younger generation, and its business of copying down and transmitting the records of the past.

In a sense, wisdom in Israel recapitulated the development already experienced in Egypt and in Babylonia. The oldest parts of the Book of Proverbs are made up of two large collections of brief sayings, put together for the most part without order or sequence; each saying or proverb states a general principle of life or some observed idiosyncrasy of human behavior. There are also translations and adaptations from Egyptian and Arabic sources. This is wisdom writing on a fairly elementary level, and it may have remained the chief style of the king's scribes and sages down until the Exile.

With the destruction of Jerusalem and its temple in 586 B.C., and the deportation of its citizens and officials to Babylonia, the Davidic monarchy came to an end. But the scribes, as a class, did not disappear along with the institutions—palace and temple—that had patronized them. On the contrary, they advanced to new importance. From being servants of the king they became doctors of the law. They found a new function and a loftier vocation in copying, enlarging, and commenting on the body of tradition that henceforth more than ever was to determine the ethos and character of Judaism: the books of the Mosaic law.

But also, they did not abandon their traditional study of wisdom; in fact, the bulk of Israel's sapiential literature as we know it comes from postexilic times. The later sections of Proverbs, especially Chapters 1 to 9, that supreme masterpiece the Book of Job, the radical questionings of Ecclesiastes, the wisdom psalms, the later books, such as Ben Sira, Wisdom of Solomon, and Baruch: all or practically all come from the five centuries following the fall of Jerusalem. The tradition, of course, by no means died out in Christian times. Matthew's gospel, for instance, contains sapiential material, notably the form known as the beatitude. The Epistle of James is a typical piece of wisdom writing, adapted to the Christian gospel but also greatly indebted to Ben Sira. And within Judaism proper a treatise such as *Pirque Aboth* continues much of the tradition of the sages.

Such in very brief outline is the history of the wisdom tradition in ancient Israel and in the cultures that mainly influenced her. We now come to the theological problem that was involved here, and how it was solved.

Wisdom literature was thoroughly secular, in its origin and essence. It arose among a class of men who were not professionally concerned with religion, with mythology or ritual. The scribes were masters of writing, that is, of a purely humanistic skill, an invention which could be turned to religious purposes but was in itself a product of human ingenuity and propagated by human pedagogy. And that also was how they thought of wisdom. They claimed for it only the authority of human experience and natural insight. To bring in arguments from mythology or ritual or any superhuman source of knowledge would be to trespass on the ground of priest or soothsayer. The scribes and sages were normally laymen. Even if, as might happen, a scribe were also a priest in the service of some god, and attached to some temple, when he composed sapiential works he set aside his religious allegiance and wrote only in terms that would be valid for all men, no matter what gods they served and by what rites. It would not, of course, be correct to think of this wisdom as atheistic. Far from it. The sages are worshipers of specific gods, and they take for granted a divine governance of the universe and the existence of moral principles and moral values. But that—apart from the subject matter of ethics —is not their proper field. The mythology of a specific worship would be a disturbing and cramping element in their discussions, and they limit their religious references to generalities.

This detachment from specific religious ties provided the wisdom of the ancient Near East with its strong note of universalism. It was addressed to all men on the common level of human experience within that particular culture. And connected with this was its second peculiar note, internationalism. The scribes ignored national frontiers, political allegiances, and dynastic conflicts or rivalries. There is little, except for minor cultural details, in a Babylonian wisdom writing that would not be comprehensible and acceptable to contemporary Egyptians, and vice versa. And there was in fact a surprising amount of cultural interchange, of translations and adaptations, in the field of wisdom literature, during the period of the so-called "first internationalism," the flourishing and sophisticated culture of the Middle Bronze Age, at the end of the third and beginning of the second millennia B.C.

It is interesting to see anticipated here the international republic of the intellect, the commonwealth of scholars, which has provided a salutary counterpart to nationalism at many periods since then.

But what place could such a neutral universalist doctrine find in the ethos of Israel? It seems at first to be a negation of the very values that constituted Israel's uniqueness and individuality. We might think that the practice and pedagogy characteristic of the sages would have been violently rejected by the authorized guardians of Israel's tradition, above all by the prophets, as an abandonment of the covenant.

It is true there are isolated criticisms of the fallibility of human wisdom and the presumption of sages here and there in the prophetic writings. But there is nothing like a general condemnation, and in fact the Israelites in general seem to have felt no such scruples. The acquisition of wisdom—I mean in the technical sense of introducing the study and practice of this literary form—seems to have struck them as part of the process of growing up, of becoming civilized, of taking their place among the other nations of the time. Naively, they glorify Solomon by the claim that he was *even* wiser than the greatest sages of the Arabs, and they picture the visiting queen from the far-distant land of Sheba as being impressed above all by his wisdom, so that "there was no spirit left in her." When the scribes of Israel began to practice and develop this new-found skill, they remained faithful for centuries to the established conventions of the genre. They do of course use the name of Israel's God, Yahweh, and hence suppose monotheism; they express the morality, with both its strength and its weaknesses, of the Mosaic code of laws. But they leave aside all that is specific and dynamic in the religion of Israel. They make no mention of Israel's special covenant with God. They have nothing to say of the Davidic monarchy as such (though they ofter refer to the duties of a king, and duties to a king). They have no doctrine of a future salvation, no eschatology, no expectation of a radical change in human existence. They say nothing, or practically nothing, about cult or about sacrificial worship, about dietary laws, or circumcision, or the observance of the sabbath, which nevertheless were such prominent practices in their own lives. In short, they remain conscientiously within their own terms of reference as wise men—very much, let us say, as a Christian scientist nowadays, writing on a scientific subject, confines himself to scientific methods and arguments and excludes as irrelevant and out of place any reference to his own belief in creation or divine providence or a future destiny of man.

But if that situation had remained unchanged, there would have been no reason to preserve the wisdom writings as part of the religious heritage of Israel. Although, as I said, they show at least negative adaptation to Israel's beliefs—for instance, in excluding reference to any god other than Yahweh—yet in their earliest stages they cannot be said to have enriched the specific tradition of Israel. What is fascinating to observe is the overriding force of the covenant faith, of the concept of the covenant God. Slowly but ineluctably that faith takes control of this originally alien philosophy and as it were compels it into its service, and the result is that the philosophy contributes notably to the development of the faith itself.

As a preliminary, let us consider the Book of Job. The author, who wished to correct the current oversimplified doctrine of retribution, to demonstrate that the relationship of man to God cannot be adequately explained on the sole basis of retributive justice, is careful to isolate his parable from the complications of the covenant doctrine. He makes use of an old piece of folklore for the outline of his story, and thus he situates his hero completely outside the people of Israel. Job is an eastern Arab, and he lives in the period of the patriarchs, long before the time of Moses. He and his friends speak of God only by the old titles of El, Eloah, and Shaddai, never Yahweh.* This

---

* The one exception within the dialogue is in Job 12:9b, but this is a quotation (from Is. 41:20).

is entirely in accord with the internationalism of wisdom writing. At the same time, no one but a believing Israelite could have written such a book. In prologue and epilogue, the author does speak of Yahweh, and thus establishes his identity with the one God of these old monotheists. Above all, the religion and faith of the hero, the author's mouthpiece, are such as no Arab, no Babylonian, no Gentile of that period, to our knowledge, ever approached. The revelation that man's attitude toward God can be a return of love for love, that a merely contractual relationship is insufficient, in fact unacceptable, that God's love may demand suffering and thereby enable man to give something to God: these sublimities rest implicitly on the doctrine of divine love that underlies the concept of covenant.

A more explicit combination of the wisdom style with the doctrine of Yahwism may be seen in what are called the wisdom psalms. These bring the vocabulary, concepts, and speculations of the sages into immediate contact with the covenant religion and attempt to solve the problems of existence in terms of the personal saving activity of Israel's God. Thus in the naive yet very beautiful Psalm 37:

> Do not be indignant about the wicked,
>   nor scandalized because of evildoers.
> For like grass they quickly wither;
>   like the green growth they fade away. . . .
> Commit your case to Yahweh;
>   trust in him and he will act.
> He will make your justice shine like light,
>   your just cause like the noonday sun.

Other psalms such as 49 and 73 are more argumentative, and go deeper into the problem of evil than this. However, though the attempt is made to supply answers to the sapiential problems from an outside source, namely, revelation, still in these psalms human wisdom and divine announcement are not really integrated.

For that to be achieved, another step was required, and this we see exemplified in the famous eighth chapter of Proverbs. Spontaneously, Israel's thinkers argued thus. If wisdom is such an estimable treasure, so precious to men, so important for all right action, then it cannot belong exclusively or even primarily to the human world. It is imparted from on high, and the real possessor of wisdom in the fullest sense is the Lord himself. He must have his own wisdom, vastly superior to any that man can claim. Mankind can acquire or receive only reflections or derivations of the wisdom that belongs to God.

Hence we see the personification of divine wisdom, describing herself as the agent by which Yahweh has accomplished his marvelous works. The passage begins like another creation story, with the positing of precreation nothingness; what is new is that even then Yahweh's wisdom was present with him.

> When there was no deep ocean, I was brought forth,
>   when there were no fountains of water;
> before the mountains were founded,
>   earlier than the hills I was brought forth,
> when as yet he had not made the earth and the fields,
>   nor the first elements of the world.

She goes on:

> When he established the sky I was present . . .
>   when he established the foundations of the earth . . .
> I was beside him as a master workman;
>   I was his delight day by day,
>   playing before him all the time,
>   playing with his world,
>   and finding my delight in the children of men.

The last line is important, because the author of this chapter of Proverbs is emphasizing the desire of this divine wisdom to communicate herself. There is nothing esoteric about her; she is not a secret possession that God jealously guards, or permits only to a few privileged initiates. No, in accord with Israel's conception of Yahweh's abundant generosity to his creatures, this most precious of his gifts is freely offered and urged upon them.

> Beside the gates that lead to the city,
>     in the entrances, Wisdom cries aloud:
> "To you, O men, I call;
>     my appeal is to the sons of men."

No other group of sapiential writers, among Israel's neighbors, had reached this remarkable conception of the divine wisdom offering itself to men for their benefit. And we notice there is no mention of Israel in these passages: it is to the children of men that the invitation is addressed.

The final step in this domestication, so to call it, of the wisdom doctrine by Israel is seen in two books of the so-called Apocrypha, or Deutero-canonica, from the last two centuries B.C. Ben Sira, or Ecclesiasticus, sums up and brings up to date all that had been the traditional thinking in Israel on the subject of wisdom, in the little encyclopedia that he published about the beginning of the second century B.C. And it was he, as far as we can tell, who achieved the final synthesis and drew together, by a logical conclusion, the doctrine of divine wisdom and the doctrine of Israel's covenant. He expressly declares that this treasure of wisdom, sought for so long and ardently by the sages of many nations, is in fact identical with Yahweh's revelation to the Israelite people.

> All this is the book of the covenant of the Most High God,
>     the law which Moses ordained for us,
>     the heritage of the congregations of Jacob.
>                                         (Ecclus. 24:23.)

He introduces Wisdom describing her own origins:

> I came forth from the mouth of the Most High;
>     like a mist I covered the earth . . .

I was in control of the waves of the sea, of the whole earth,
  of every people and race.
Among all these I sought a resting place;
  in whose territory should I lodge?
Then the creator of all gave me his command;
  he who created me fixed my dwelling.
He said, "Pitch your tent in Jacob,
  have your heritage in Israel . . ."
And thus I was established in Sion;
  my government is in Jerusalem;
I have my roots among a glorified people,
  in the Lord's property, and his heritage.

(Ecclus. 24:3–12.)

This was indeed a radical step, and to us at first sight
it may seem an unfortunate narrowing down of the earlier
more liberal, universalist concept. But it would not be
fair so to regard it. The law that Ben Sira has in mind is
not the rigid code of external observances, fenced in by
an elaborate casuistry, that we associate with later Rab-
binic teaching. Ben Sira shows no interest in the minutiae
of external regulations. He is thinking of the whole revelation granted to Israel, which made known the character
and will of the one true God, and required of Israelites a
certain moral way of life, as a response. In the second
century B.C., both revelation and response were increasingly being made available to Gentiles. It is not a narrowing but a heightening of wisdom that he proclaims, one
that had already been hinted at in the motto of the Book
of Proverbs, "the beginning of wisdom is the fear of
Yahweh." The fear, yir'ah, is a term that includes reverence, obedience, even a filial love, all shown in a loyal
living out of the relationship graciously bestowed by God.
Ben Sira, as was inevitable, is mainly concerned with his
own people; he has no mission to the Gentiles. But the
universalism affirmed, sporadically but with great emphasis, in the prophetical literature was still a living part
of the tradition, and Israel's possessions and privileges

were destined some day to be communicated to the rest of mankind.

On the other hand, Ben Sira is immeasurably enriching the concept of wisdom itself. What had started out as a purely human invention, the acquisition of certain skills, had been raised by earlier Israelite sages to denote a transcendent divine attribute. Now Ben Sira points out how this divine possession has been sent down to men. They are not limited now to human wisdom such as was developed by the Gentiles. They have access, through revelation, to the infinitely higher wisdom of God himself.

The other late composition, from a time soon after that of Ben Sira, is the Book of Baruch; its middle section sums up with great beauty and eloquence the place of wisdom in Israel's faith. It repeats Ben Sira's doctrine, and it also uses this doctrine to answer the questions of the passage from Job that was quoted at the beginning of this chapter.

After describing the failure of the search for true wisdom by all generations of the heathen, by the ancient kings and legendary giants, by the sons of Hagar who seek for understanding on the earth, by the storytellers and the searchers after insight, it goes on:

> Who has gone up to heaven and taken her,
>> and brought her down from the clouds? . . .
> There is no one who knows the way to her,
>> or understands her paths.
> Only the one who knows all things knows her,
>> has discovered her through his understanding . . .
> He has discovered the whole way to knowledge,
>> has bestowed it on Jacob his servant,
>> on Israel, his beloved. . . .
> This is the book of the commandments of God,
>> the law, that endures forever . . .
> Happy are we, Israel,
>> because the things that please God are known to us.
>> (Bar. 3:29–4:4.)

Those quotations will suffice for this brief survey. It has shown one very typical example of the assimilative power of the Israelite tradition. As in so many other fields of intellectual and religious interest, the Yahwist theologians, in their successive generations, took over the ideas, the traditions, and the institutions of other peoples and with supreme confidence and insight adapted them to their own covenant belief. The work did not remain a merely negative purification, a leaving aside of discordant elements. Israel's lofty doctrine proved to be a fertilizing influence upon the thought of the Gentiles, developing it to new heights of understanding and enlightenment. Even from the literary and cultural points of view, a comparative examination of ancient sapiential literatures will establish the unmistakable superiority of the level of insight attained in Israel. This may be confirmed quite pragmatically, by comparing the profit and inspiration to be derived by any modern reader from the wisdom of Israel with those likely to be gained from that of other peoples. Finally, for the believing reader there is here contained another stage in divine revelation, an illuminating doctrine that is not to be found in the historical books or in the writings of the prophets. The Christian sees this long development as a preparation for the doctrine proclaimed by St. Paul, when he names Christ the Wisdom of God.

Chapter 7

## The Prayer of Israel

AS HAS BEEN STRESSED more than once already, all the religions that men have ever practiced offer some form of salvation, promise some well-being that cannot be achieved or assured by men's own unaided efforts. This is just as true of revealed religions as of "natural" religions. The Christian believer sees a distinctive mark of his belief, not in the mere fact that it does hold out a promise and a hope, but in the fact that the salvation thus proposed is of a kind that man could never have thought of by himself. It surpasses natural dreams and aspirations. It lies on a higher plane. It consists in an intimate and eternal union of the believer with a personal and loving God. There are other creeds that promise union with a divinity, or perhaps one should say with the Divine, with the All-Being that alone is real and enduring; but those lofty faiths do not present divinity as a person, with a thought, a will, and a love.

These conceptions of the personality of God, and of the transcendence of the salvation he promises, are naturally reflected in the prayer that is addressed to him. Prayer—the speech, in the widest sense, addressed by men to the divinity they worship—is one of the best keys to understanding what they truly think of him, or it. Where texts of prayers are available, and can be securely interpreted, they are a surer guide to the thoughts and sentiments of the general membership of a religion than is a mythology, or the official statements of belief, where such exist. These last, for example, are drawn up by religious leaders, whose theology may be a good deal in advance of popular religious ideas. But the prayers which are composed for public liturgical use may be presumed, as a general rule, to give apt expression to the sentiments, the beliefs, the hopes and fears, of the worshipers as a group. They tell us much, in particular, both by statement and by implication, about the divinity concerned, and they express most vividly what is expected of him—what kind of salvation the people hope to receive from his benevolence, and on what grounds they hope for it.

Of course, where prayers of petition are concerned, not much variety is to be looked for in the favors requested. The long catalogue of human needs and cravings shows little fundamental variation from one religion's documents to another's. Always there are the same boons to be sought: abundant food, the birth of children, the warding off of sickness and poverty, and in general the achievement of man's fallacious and shortsighted projects. And there are the same sufferings to be relieved, the same calamities to be remedied: illness and the threat of death, hunger and destitution, humiliation or destruction by enemies, in short, the thwarting of man's best laid plans. These appeals assure us only of the essential sameness of human nature, the recurring threats to man's security and happiness, and the constant belief that help in these matters can be sought from suprahuman powers.

On the other hand, specific religious differences occur in prayers of praise which directly invoke these powers, and in those sections of the prayers of petition which put forward reasons why the deity should make a benevolent response. Such invocation and motivation are conditioned by the mental image which the worshipers have formed of their God, and by their understanding of their relationship to him. As we should expect, it is in these respects that Israelite prayers are distinguished from those of the Canaanites, the Aramaeans, the Babylonians, and the rest. All of them sought divine aid against life's afflictions, and divine blessing on their activities. Where they differed was in their concept of the divinities they addressed, and the arguments by which they sought to move them.

Our main source for the prayer of Israel is naturally the Psalter, the large collection of mainly liturgical texts which was accumulated, by a careful process of selection and editing, over perhaps six centuries, in connection with the sacrificial worship in the temple of Jerusalem. A large nucleus of this collection dates from before the Exile, but many postexilic compositions are also included; its final editing must have been completed by about the third century B.C. Besides the Psalter, there are two other collections of poems in the canon: Lamentations, and the Canticle of Canticles. The former at least has certainly a liturgical destination. Finally, scattered through the historical and prophetic books are a fair number of other prayers, the older ones prevailing in poetic form, the later postexilic compositions usually in prose. Thus we have a considerable thesaurus of compositions on which to base a judgment of the tone and content of the liturgical prayer of Israel.

Broadly speaking, we may group these prayers under two heads: praise and petition. The praise is expressed in hymns and in psalms of thanksgiving, the petitions in what are called the laments, and the psalms of penitence. Let us consider first the form of praise.

Hymns of praise, acclamations, celebrations of a god's glory, goodness, and power, were usual features of the religions of the time. Marduk was praised in Babylon, Assur in Nineveh, Dagon in Gaza—all in formal hymns celebrating their great achievements and manifold powers. What is the motivation that inspires this particular form of worship, which seems directed to the glory of the god alone, and without tangible profit or result for the worshipers? Is it the idea of flattery—that because men are pleased by adulation, the god will likewise be flattered by this proclamation of his greatness, and so be more disposed to listen favorably to the petitions that are to follow? That, it seems to me, is a shallow and quite inadequate analysis of the mental processes here at work, even among the Gentile religions, and still more in Israel. In the latter, at least, the acclamation of Yahweh is a simple obligation for his covenant partners. It is the required human response in the dialogue that Yahweh has initiated with this community. He has spoken to them, through his servant Moses, through the prophets, and through his great historical actions on their behalf. That speech requires an answer: not only the substantive answer of lives lived in accordance with the stipulations of the covenant, the commandments, but the ceremonial answer of acclamation in a cult.

That cult of course was sacrificial. The system of animal sacrifices in honor of Yahweh was practiced in Jerusalem for over a thousand years, apart from a seventy-year interruption when the temple lay in ruins. But that technique was shared by Yahwism with practically all the other sedentary religions of the period, and sacrifice as such has nothing specific about it. We shall consider therefore only the texts that accompanied the sacrifices and distinguished those of Israel from all others. We cannot now witness the liturgy performed in the Solomonic temple or in the postexilic temple that succeeded it; but from the psalms we can form some idea of this religion in action, of what the worshipers did, and even of what they thought and felt while they were doing it.

For an example of the hymn, I may quote in its entirety Psalm 117, the shortest in the Psalter:

> Praise Yahweh, all you nations;
>     acclaim him, all you peoples;
> for great is his covenant love for us,
>     and Yahweh's faithfulness endures forever.

Here is the regular hymnal style. First the summons, an imperative in the second person plural, to praise Yahweh, who is spoken of only in the third person. Then the human motivation for this imperative is added, the reasons why Yahweh must be praised. These are taken from the covenant doctrine: he deserves acclaim because of his loyal and dependable help to Israel, in accordance with the covenant relationship he has graciously bestowed on her. What seems strange is that not merely Israel should praise him on this account, but "all you nations" and "all you peoples." Right here we have a compressed but very clear testimony to the universalism that was always at least latent in Yahwism. This particular and limited covenant somehow, sometime, was to issue in a great blessing upon the whole race of men. (This was foreshadowed, as we saw, even in the tradition of the promise to Abraham.)

Originally, no doubt, this type of hymnal summons was addressed to the assembly of those physically present in the court of the temple, as in Psalm 118:1-4, where, in succession, the laity, the priests, and the Gentile proselytes are called on to utter in chorus the word of praise. But the summons could also be addressed to the absent nations, as in the above quotation, or to the inanimate creation, as in Isaiah 44:23.

> Sing, you heavens, for Yahweh has acted;
>     shout, you depths of the earth!
> Break into singing, you mountains,
>     the forest, and every tree therein.
> For Yahweh has redeemed Jacob
>     and is revealing his glory in Israel.

Or, in a more personal and individual vein, it could even be addressed to oneself.

> Bless Yahweh, my soul;
>     let all that is in me bless his holy name.
> Bless Yahweh, my soul,
>     and forget not all his loving benefits. (Ps. 103:1-2.)

The motivation also developed and was varied. Yahweh's acts in fulfillment of the covenant were always primary reasons. But as the awareness of his creative activity developed, his cosmic functions too were cited as reasons for praise. We find both motives combined in Psalm 95, which is the hymn accompanying a procession into the temple area. Verses 3 to 5 describe Yahweh as Lord of creation:

> For Yahweh is a great God,
>     a great king over all the gods;
> in his hand are the depths of the earth;
>     the heights of the mountains are his too;
> the sea is his, for he made it,
>     and the dry land, which his hands shaped.

Then, after renewed summons, verse 7 describes him as Lord of the covenant:

> For he is our God,
>     and we the people of his pasture,
>     the sheep under his hand.

Thanksgivings, whether public or private, come under the general heading of praise, but with two formal differences: in them Yahweh is usually directly addressed in the second person; and the motivation naturally includes some particular benefit or answer to prayer. Often the whole story is narrated, of the sufferer's danger and distress, the prayer he uttered, and Yahweh's prompt salvation. Thus, Psalm 30:

> I will praise you, Yahweh, for you rescued me;
>     you did not let my enemies exult over me.
> Yahweh, my God, I cried to you for help,
>     and you healed me.
> Yahweh, you have brought me up from the underworld,
>     brought me back to life from among those who go
>         down into the pit. . . .
> You have turned my mourning into joy,
>     put off my sackcloth and clothed me with gladness,
> so that I can sing your praises without ceasing:
>     Yahweh, my God, I will praise you forever.

These quotations may suffice to illustrate the complete realism, one might say the pragmatism, of Israel's prayer. Yahweh is the most real thing in the lives of this people.

They have collectively experienced his activities on their behalf, and individually they have particular benefits to thank him for. They do it enthusiastically but also matter-of-factly.

But there are also petitions to be uttered, when Yahweh's salvation is desired but has not yet materialized. Then he must be notified, so to speak, that his intervention is called for. Again motivation must be added, in this case, divine motivation, reasons why he ought to act. These consist, first of all, in appeals to his character as a God of salvation. He is that kind of God, and they need only remind him of it. Thus the collective petition in Psalm 80:

> O Shepherd of Israel, listen to us!
>   you who guide Joseph like a flock;
> enthroned upon the cherubim,
>   shine forth before Ephraim, Benjamin, Manasse.
> Exert your power,
>   and come, bring us salvation.
> Yahweh, restore us!
>   let your face shine out, that we may be saved.

Other reasons may be cited, some of which may strike us as naive:

> To you, Yahweh, I cried out;
>   to the Lord I cried for mercy:
> "What profit is there in my blood,
>   if I go down to the pit?
> Will dust praise you?
>   Will it declare your faithfulness?
> Hear, Yahweh, and have pity on me;
>   Yahweh, be my helper." (Ps. 30:9–11.)

The possible obstacles to enjoying the benefits which in the normal course of things Yahweh provides include such afflictions as sickness, destitution, threatened lawsuits or judicial condemnations, the machinations of personal enemies, imprisonment, exile. There are special psalms composed to implore relief from all these various calamities. But one obstacle was of a peculiar kind, and of this the prayer of Israel is always more or less conscious: namely, sin. Infidelity, disobedience, or ingratitude—rejection of the covenant in any form—interposes an impassable barrier to Yahweh's salvation. Where the petitioner is conscious of sin, it somehow must be removed before the rest of his petition has any chance of being received.

It is the paradox of sin, as the Israelite sees it, that man can commit it, can bring it into being, but cannot remove or undo it. Only God can do that. The sinner has set in motion a fatal force that will inevitably destroy him—unless Yahweh himself, in his mercy and condescension, is willing to interfere. And here, in what are called the psalms of penitence, we have perhaps the most profound and most impressive of Israel's prayers. Here Yahweh's saving activity is seen at its highest. Freely, he forgives men, receives them back into his favor; and he takes active steps to cleanse them, to destroy the evil reality which otherwise would hound them to destruction. It is clear that the Israelites did not, so to speak, moralize sin. They thought of it as something very real and objective, which would normally produce disastrous effects. But they were saved from any too materialist or superstitious concepts of sin, by seeing it always in essence as a personal offense against a personal God. And though he could allow them to endure many of its fatal effects, he could also if he chose suspend and remove these.

It is hardly necessary to quote at length. The famous Psalm 51 may serve as illustration:

> Have pity on me, Yahweh, in your covenant love;
>    in your abundant mercy wipe out my transgression.
> Wash my guilt completely away,
>    and cleanse me from my sin.

For I am conscious of my transgressions;
    my sin is always before me.
Against you, you alone, have I sinned,
    and done what is evil in your sight . . .
Create for me a clean heart, Yahweh;
    renew a faithful spirit within me.
Do not drive me out of your presence;
    do not take away from me your holy spirit. . . .
A broken and contrite heart,
    Yahweh, you will not despise.

Another example may be quoted from one of the many collective penitential psalms of the postexilic period. This is found in Isaiah, Chapters 63 and 64, and it begins, "Yahweh's acts of love I will recount." It goes on to contrast with this love Israel's ungraciousness and disloyalty. For these the community have suffered terrible punishment; now the time has come for God to forgive them.

Look down from the heavens, and see,
    from the height of your holiness and glory.
Where are your zeal, your power,
    your tender pity and your compassion?
Hold back no longer—you are our father . . .
    our redeemer for all time—that is your name. . . .
Yes, you were angry at our sins;
    through our misdeeds we incurred guilt.
We have all become like a thing unclean,
    all our righteous deeds like a filthy rag.
We all wither like leaves;
    like the wind our guilt sweeps us away. . . .
You have hidden your face from us,
    and delivered us up to our sins.
Yet still, Yahweh, you are our father;
    we are the clay, you are the potter . . .
Be not angry, Yahweh, beyond measure,
    nor remember our guilt forever.

Such texts may serve as a corrective to an oversimplified view of the idea and practice of religion in ancient Israel. Israel's literature bitterly castigates the people's infidelity, idolatry, immorality; and it is easy to think, in reading some of the prophets' fulminations, that this curious people, with so lofty an idea of God and such a fixation on their religious beliefs, were nevertheless, perversely, the most wicked of all nations. But in so judging, we should be unfairly exploiting Israel's own frank confession. There was a higher level of morality and worship in ancient Israel than in the surrounding nations, and even in her darkest periods of corruption, so unsparingly condemned by the prophets, there remained this current of sincere devotion represented by the psalms and other prayers. The prophets were not such isolated figures as we may be tempted to think. The psalms show us how Israel thought about God, how sensitive her conscience was; and there was always the faithful remnant, at least, that had not bowed the knee to Baal. The psalms expressed the religion and nourished the piety of these faithful ones, and the late prose prayers of books such as Daniel and Nehemiah breathe an equally touching spirit of humility, contrition, and childlike confidence and love.

Finally, there are some quite individual productions, not intended for public use, which show us how some historic members of the commonwealth of Israel reacted to the national religion. For example, we may consider the so-called "confessions" of Jeremiah, which vividly show us the prophet struggling with the intolerable tensions of his vocation, feeling himself crushed between the anvil of the people's skepticism and the hammer of the word of Yahweh:

You misled me, Yahweh, and I was deceived;
    you got the better of me, you have had your way.
I have become the butt of ridicule all day long;
    all make fun of me. . . .
Yahweh of hosts, you who test the just,
    and see into men's hearts,

let me see how you take vengeance on them,
   for I have entrusted my case to you. (Jer. 20:7–12.)

Not less intense and personal are the prayers of Job in the book of that name. It is notable that throughout the dialogue with the three friends only Job ever directly addresses a prayer to God. The friends utter eloquent hymns in praise of God; they urge Job to pray and ask pardon for his putative offenses. But they themselves— righteous, wise, secure men—feel no need to ask God for anything. Their religion is a quasi-commercial transaction; they are quite deficient in the sense of personal intimacy and communion with God which the author is concerned to demonstrate as the great virtue of his hero. Fittingly, at the end of the book, they are rebuked by this mysterious God whom they have so misunderstood, for "not having spoken rightly about me—as has my servant Job."

This personal awareness of God leads Job to address him with startling freedom:

> Am I the ocean, or the sea serpent,
>    that you should set a guard over me? . . .
> What is man, that you make so much of him,
>    and fix on him your attention,
> inspecting him every morning,
>    examining him at each moment? . . .
> Even if I have sinned, what harm could I do you,
>    you Watcher of men? (Job 7:12–20.)

> I will give vent to my complaint,
>    will express the bitterness of my soul.
> I will say to God, "Do not declare my guilt;
>    let me know what it is you accuse me of.
> Do you enjoy acting the tyrant,
>    despising the work of your hands,
>      and favoring the schemes of the wicked?"
>                         (Job 10:1–3.)

If there is one quality that should impress us in the prayers of Israel, it may well be sincerity. Refined or naive, sublime or down-to-earth, humble or impatient and vengeful—they may be all these things, but never are they insincere. And this partly explains the undying appeal and effectiveness of Israel's psalms. The truth, genuineness, and candor of these texts are unsurpassable, and all later generations have found mirrored there, and already expressed, their most secret desires and questionings and their own self-knowledge. That depth and psychological insight were evoked by the psalmists' penetrating faith in the deity whom they addressed. With him no deception would avail, no boastfulness or self-satisfaction would be tolerable. Entire devotion in his praise, and entire truthfulness in their own petitions—these were the only formulas that could be effective, that the psalmists would even dare to employ in his worship. That is why the prayer of Israel is such an extraordinary revelation, both of the nature of the God to whom Israel prayed, and of the nature of the human creatures who stand, humbly but hopefully, before him.

# Chapter 8

# The Hope in Israel's Future

THE TITLE OF this chapter is concerned with the ancient Israel of pre-Christian times; the hope referred to is the hope that was then entertained of God's future action, of definitive salvation. Thus our field of interest remains the people of God, as we find them in the world of the Old Testament. We have been considering the many distinctive characteristics of that people's culture and beliefs, all of which, as I have tried to show, depended on their peculiar and unparalleled concept of a covenant deity. The last such characteristic to be discussed is their hopefulness, their confident, forward-looking expectation that the future held something better, that a still greater salvation awaited them. This was based on their firm belief that the God who had called them was a God who made promises, and could and would keep them.

This motif of promise is absent from the other religions of that time and general area. The nature-gods or city-gods of Egypt and Babylonia made no such engagements. They were of course expected to provide the salvation that was, so to speak, their professional responsibility: blessings of fertility and good weather, of protection against plague, famine, or human enemies. At most, they would give favorable omens guaranteeing the successful outcome of some enterprise for which their assistance was sought. But it was unknown, and would have been quite out of character, that they should proclaim a program of future activity, chosen by themselves, unlimited in scope and extension.

But precisely this was what the Israelites believed about Yahweh. In the earliest traceable form of the tradition, in the stories about Abraham, we find this theme already developed. "Set out from your native land, from your people and from your family, towards the land which I will show you. I will make you into a great nation . . . all the families of the earth will bless themselves by you." The suspense of the stories about Abraham centers around the means by which the fulfillment of the promise is to be set in motion. The obstacles are heaped up, the sterility of Abraham's only legal wife, the rejection of his other sons, the demand finally for the sacrifice of Isaac: these are meant to underline how Abraham's trust in God is finally vindicated, and how well grounded was the hope to which he clung. Even the picturesque narrative, in Genesis 23, of the purchase of a burial ground at Hebron is intended to indicate the legal foothold, so to call it, that Abraham acquired in the promised land, even in his own lifetime. The post-Mosaic Israelites, who treasured these stories and recorded them in their sacred history, saw in their own existence as a numerous people, occupying the land of Canaan, the tangible fulfillment of the promise and the realization of Abraham's hope.

Similarly with the promise involved in the Sinaitic covenant. Its content had been left vague, but this was simply the convention of the suzerainty treaty from which the form of Yahweh's covenant was apparently derived. As was fitting to the great king, who graciously establishes a covenant with his inferiors, Yahweh had refrained from specifying what he would do for the people—who on their side were bound to very specific acts and the avoidance of specific crimes. But the blanket affirmation, "You shall be my people and I will be your God," is eloquent in its implications. The Israelites saw those implications worked out in their lives, in the vividly conceived presence of Yahweh in the ark, and later in the temple, in the communication of his spirit to certain inspired warriors and holy men, in the successful occupation and extension of their territory.

All those early promises to Israel, in the naive springtime of her covenant relationship, were in tangible and realistic terms; they held out expectations such as corresponded to the dearest dreams and secret longings of the people concerned. To Abraham was promised the ideal of the seminomad wanderer, the transition from nomadism to settlement, the repose on a terrain that was to be his permanent possession, with certain support from the soil and a relief from all the hazards, the incessant journeying, and the restlessness that seemed so burdensome to the wanderer. To the oppressed Semitic serfs in Egypt, Moses brought the good news of a liberation, freedom from the house of bondage, and the enjoyment by each Israelite of his own vine and fig tree, with none to call him to account. By the period of the kingship, from the tenth century on, such hopes had been largely fulfilled; yet always there was more to wish for, as the gain in material possessions and even security was offset by new complications of existence, new sources of insecurity and unrest.

The interesting development in the hope of the Israelites is the gradual raising of their sights. The combination of experience with a deepening understanding of their God slowly but steadily, over a period of a thousand years, led to an increasingly lofty and transcendent idea of what salvation really meant. Gradually we see their hope rise above the earthly level of secure and abundant material resources. At the same time there is a growing comprehension, and a spiritualization, of the obstacles that delay or impede the full bestowal of that salvation. They are seen to be internal rather than external. Not just the threat of unreliable or erratic natural processes, not only the danger from other hostile human groups: more and more, the Israelites came to see the hindrance as interior to themselves, consisting in their own fatal tendencies to resist God, to go contrary to his will, and to grab shortsightedly at the nearest human expedients, with disregard for his announced guidance and instruction. In short, the one real obstacle to their receiving from Yahweh the fullness of salvation is their own sin.

The first great step in raising their hope above a mainly naturalistic level was the mystique that attached itself very early to the figure of David. The institution of kingship already had an enormous religious prestige in the world of the time, and David's fascinating personality and romantic history, along with the speed and success of his military victories, created even in his own lifetime the myth of the superhuman nature of his rule. This may not have been universal among the people, but it was certainly fostered by the prophets and psalmists about his court. As with everything else in Israel, a specific character was given to it by Yahwism. David was the anointed of Yahweh, the king after Yahweh's heart, and Yahweh had rewarded David's loyalty with a special personal covenant, which like all his works was marked with his own indefectibility and permanence. David's dynasty therefore was to be everlasting, and—since Yahweh tended always to produce more glorious deeds in the future than he had done in the past—a future king or kings would surpass even the magnificence of David himself. This mystique radiated on all that was connected with David: his throne, his city, the ritual he developed about the ark of the covenant. Since a king needs subjects and a city needs citizens, this future glory must extend, too, to the inhabitants of Jerusalem. Not all this was worked out at once, of course, but the germ of the whole idea is in the famous oracle to David in 2 Samuel 7, which is repeated in Psalm 89.

A counterpart to this first transcendent doctrine is the realistic, pragmatic approach to salvation which we associate with Deuteronomy and the work of the Deuteronomic writers. This current of doctrine naturally does not rest its hope on the Davidic institutions, since it developed among the northern tribes who had rejected the Davidic dynasty. Instead, it harks back, with the greatest conviction and insistence, to the Mosaic tradition. It stresses the perfect fulfillment, up to date, of all Yahweh's promises; and its main purpose is to instill an absolute loyalty to the covenant, a perfect living up to Yahweh's requirements. Given that, the hope and assurance of the Deuteronomists are limited to a present, earthly horizon. Salvation is here, at hand, available to all: it consists in the idyllic and peaceful existence of the Israelites as cultivators and proprietors in Palestine, hedged around by Yahweh's unfailing protection, and lacking nothing of what constitutes the good life. Only their disloyalty or ingratitude can threaten this well-being, by provoking Yahweh to chastise and afflict them.

This doctrine is inculcated with great warmth and eloquence in the introductory chapters of Deuteronomy. The Book of Judges, as we now have it, was expressly composed to illustrate this doctrine from history, and later, when catastrophe had fallen and the communities of Israel and Judah were scattered, the Book of Kings was written to demonstrate how an ungrateful people had brought disaster on themselves.

As well as these official doctrines, there was a popular eschatology of the time, in the ninth and eighth centuries B.C., which we know of mainly by the prophets' criticism of it. Amos, about 760, preaching in the then prosperous northern kingdom of Israel, vehemently attacks the nonethical expectation of "the Day of Yahweh."

> Unhappy men, who long for the Day of Yahweh!
>   what will the Day of Yahweh mean to you?
> It will be darkness, not light.
> Like a man running away from a lion,
>   only to be met by a bear.     (Amos 5:18–19.)

The popular hope, then, was in an intervention of Yahweh which should manifest his glory by destroying all Israel's enemies—regardless of Israel's moral corruption and infidelity to Yahweh's commands. "You only have I known," says Amos in God's name, "of all the families of the earth." Therefore, the people would conclude, Yahweh must bring us salvation. "Therefore," goes on the prophet, "will I visit upon you all your iniquities."

One could illustrate this sharp rejection of corrupted religious feeling from practically all the prophetic writings. But this single quotation suffices to indicate the doctrinal dilemma that confronted the prophets. On the one hand, Yahweh's promises stood. He was a God of salvation, and over and over he had committed himself to provide all, and much more than, any other gods could offer in the way of happiness, prosperity, and peace. On the other hand, he was also a God of justice, affronted by human ingratitude, owing it to himself not to let rebellion go unpunished, not to let the sinner get away with his wickedness. In the attempt to clarify how these two apparently conflicting claims would work out, that great religious thinker whom we know as Isaiah appealed to the doctrine of the remnant—which in fact had already been exemplified in the ancient Israelite tradition of the Flood. If—as seemed to the prophet—the people as a whole were stubbornly irreformable, were by their actions declaring the covenant to be null and void, then they would be given over to destruction. But Yahweh's fidelity and love would still find material to act on, in a faithful minority that could be picked out from among the people. This limiting of salvation to a remnant, who by innocence or at least by repentance were capable of receiving it, was, paradoxically, a step in the direction of universalism. It tended to detach the religion of ancient Israel from its identification with one ethnic and national group, and to substitute the personal requirement of faith and loyalty to Israel's God for the physical qualification of being children of Abraham.

In the century following Isaiah, the dilemma between Yahweh's will to save, and Israel's unwillingness to be saved, grew ever sharper. The great and tragic figure of Jeremiah and the fierce, eccentric Ezekiel were faced with it in its keenest form, as they witnessed the disaster that had been so insistently foretold by their predecessors and by themselves. In 586 B.C. the Davidic monarchy was swept away, the city of Jerusalem destroyed, the temple itself demolished; and most of the surviving citizens became deportees and exiles in Babylonia. What now was the hope of Israel?

It is most impressive to see how tenaciously this hope was reaffirmed. We receive a vivid impression of the psychological shock, the sense of an event utterly unthinkable, from the contemporary Book of Lamentations. Though this is now associated with the name of Jeremiah, it was in fact composed by writers who had little in common with the prophet's outlook, who simply had not believed him. They are dumbfounded at the verification of his judgments on king, city, and people. Yet their faith in Yahweh is unshaken by it all. They must violently readjust their thinking, and they do so, to admit that Yahweh, after all, was not compelled for his name's sake to protect a city regardless of its inhabitants' behavior, that this disaster was due only to man's stubborn incomprehension, and that the prophets, after all, had been telling the truth. And if they have, then Israel can still hope. By asserting the doctrine of the remnant, both Jeremiah and Ezekiel had affirmed that the relationship between Yahweh and his people was not broken for good. Hosea had foreseen the restoration of the covenant, after infidelity, punishment, and repentance. Jeremiah and Ezekiel prefer to picture it as a new covenant, different in several important respects from the old. To break the fatal downward spiral of human infidelity, Yahweh must work an interior change in the humanity that he allies with himself. Jeremiah puts it thus: "I will make a new covenant with the house of Israel, not like the covenant which I made with their fathers . . . I will put my law within them and I will write it on their hearts" (Jer. 31:31–33). And Ezekiel: "I will give you a new heart and will put a new spirit within you. I will remove your stony hearts out of your bodies, and will give you hearts of flesh; and I will put my spirit within you" (Ezek. 36:26–27). An inner reformation, worked by Yahweh's spirit, is to purify and rectify the heart of Israel, which had shown itself so persistently unresponsive to God's love. Only when thus transformed and re-created could a human group respond as they should to divine love and run no risk of nullifying the covenant by their own willfulness.

Henceforth the Israelites never forgot this lesson. Their sinfulness and guilt, personal and ancestral, became a pervading theme, almost to excess, in the postexilic literature. But always there was room for hope, because the mercy and faithfulness of Yahweh were present, to be set off against that dark background. Every step of recovery from the near annihilation of the Exile was welcomed as another evident fulfillment of Yahweh's promise to forgive and to restore. The rapturous proclamations of Second Isaiah, as he saw the time of Jerusalem's restoration approaching, are so many summonses to reviving hope:

> Why do you say, O Jacob,
>     why do you claim, O Israel,
> "My way is hidden from Yahweh;
>     my defense is neglected by my God"?
> Have you not realized?
>     Have you not heard?
> Yahweh is a God everlasting,
>     creator of the ends of the earth. (Is. 40:27–28.)

> Remember these things, O Jacob,
>     Israel, for you are my servant.
> I formed you; you are my servant,
>     Israel, not to be forgotten by me.
> I have blown away your transgressions like mist,
>     your sins, like a cloud.
> Return to me, for I have redeemed you. (Is. 44:21–22.)

Second Isaiah's own firm hope is linked to the city of Jerusalem, which for him takes the place held for the first Isaiah by the Davidic kingship. The rebuilding of the temple, the restoration of the citizenry, the re-establishment of the physical city with gates and fortifications—all these things followed within the century and served as further confirmations of the solidity of Israel's tenacious hope. Yet another of the prophet's visions concerned the universalism of the salvation that was to be worked, the seeking of the Gentiles for instruction and peace. This was connected with his most profound insight, that the agent of this universalism was to be a specially chosen servant of Yahweh, who in perfect submission and obedience should fulfill his master's plan, even to the sacrificing of his own life, and then be restored, glorified, and rewarded by his triumphant success in the evangelization of the Gentiles.

This brings us to the ultimate form that the hope of Israel took. The political weakness and complete subjection of the postexilic community had their effects certainly upon the "shape of things to come" as that community envisaged them. In the fifth and fourth centuries B.C. Judea was a small frontier province of the Persian empire, administered by a local governor who was responsible to the satrap of Syria. There is no trace of an attempted recovery of political independence, or even of a serious move in that direction. Chastened, poverty-stricken, comparatively few in numbers, the Jews of the Return concentrated their forces within the community, cultivated their own religious life as intensely as they could, and were content to "wait upon the Lord" and to leave to him the further restoration —and expansion—that must be still to come. A preparation for the latter was perhaps the growing Diaspora, the widely scattered Jewish community that lived outside Palestine, among, yet not a part of, Gentile populations. Its members for the most part remained fiercely loyal to their ancestral religion, observed its external requirements as they were then interpreted, and kept in touch with the cradle of their faith by visits or at least by monetary contributions to the temple. It was understood that when the day of the Lord came they all would return to Jerusalem, and there be ready to receive the humbled survivors of the Gentiles, who would come begging for crumbs from the table of Israel.

It was in this setting that apocalypses arose. This is the vivid expression of Israel's faith in the future activity of her God, in its purest form. The Israelites had despaired of their own human resources, and anyway Yahweh needed nothing of that kind to overthrow the presumptuous and insolent powers of this world, and to introduce his divine and everlasting kingdom. No longer did Israel feel called on to fight the battles of the Lord. In patience and in hope his people would await his decision that the time was come, they would be spectators of the coming upheaval of heaven and earth, and after the great judgment they would joyfully take the privileged positions that awaited them, in the kingdom of God.

This is the teaching of the greatest of the Jewish apocalypses, the second half of the Book of Daniel. Called forth by the struggle between the would-be Hellenizers and the guardians of tradition, after 170 B.C., a struggle in which the former were supported by the power of the Gentile monarch Antiochus IV, the book pictures this conflict (a matter of life and death, as it turned out, for the existence of Judaism) as a reflection in earthly politics of the cosmic battle between the forces of good and evil. Certainly, inevitably, the former would triumph, because Yahweh was fighting for them. But the author of Daniel does not urge military action, for example, the following of Judas Maccabeus, who raised the standard of revolt and took to guerrilla warfare just at that time. In human terms, the apocalyptist is a pacifist. He has no other recommendations to make than entire fidelity to the law of God, and if necessary the courageous facing of martyrdom. The faithful have nothing to do but to *remain* faithful: they can leave it to the Lord in his own good time to vindicate his holy ones, to overthrow their persecutors, and to establish his everlasting kingdom. This thoroughgoing transcendentalism, curiously enough, is not in the least pessimistic or gloomy. On the contrary, the Book of Daniel fairly glows with a conviction and a hope, one might say, a joy, in the ultimate act of salvation seen as so close at hand. There is only a little time to wait. And those who have been put to death in the meantime, who have maintained their loyalty even to death, will not be cheated out of the reward. They will be gloriously raised from the dead, their bodies restored to life, to take part with their surviving companions in God's final triumph.

This apocalyptic attitude is the final form that the hope of Israel took before the Christian era. The exploits of the Maccabees, their achievement of nearly a century of political independence, their short-lived restoration of a powerful Jewish kingdom in Palestine, were seen to have little religious significance, once the temple had been purified and the cult restored. The Hasmonean kingdom was too obviously another dynastic power, devoid in practice of religious sanction, and actually antagonizing the chief religious elements among the people. Sects multiplied and proliferated; holy men appeared, announcing various messages and doctrines concerning the proximate appearance of the kingdom of God. One such was the Teacher of Righteousness, who established down by the Dead Sea the sect whose library is now giving us such a welcome and unexpected glimpse into first-century Judaism. In general, the expectation was of some great and unmistakable divine intervention, which should fulfill all the promises of the prophets and justify all the long-drawn-out hope and expectation of Israel.

Was the hope of Israel realized? Or was it vain? Or is it still awaiting realization? Different answers are naturally offered to these questions. I have no competence or title to speak for modern Israel, or to indicate what answers would be given by her. It is in place here only to set forth, very briefly, the fulfillment that was claimed for that hope, and is claimed today, by the Christian Church.

The early Church appears first as a Jewish sect, inhabiting Jerusalem, and announcing a peculiar good news about its founder. Very soon, it is found to be in opposition to the official organs of Judaism; displaced and driven abroad, it rapidly develops into a mainly Gentile group. Its preaching, however, continues to lay stress on its essential connection with Israel's history and Israel's beliefs. Concerning its founder, it makes these claims: All the prophecies were fulfilled, and all the hopes of Israel realized, in the coming of Jesus of Nazareth, who proclaimed himself both son of Man and son of God. He is of the line of David, and is presented as the Davidic king. He is the servant of Yahweh, carrying out with entire fidelity the program Israel had not performed, of evangelizing the Gentiles, and sacrificing himself in the process. He teaches a doctrine that includes all that Israel believed, with further depths of explanation such as Israel had longed for. He calls Yahweh his father, and he understands this in no such metaphoric sense as would apply to Israel but as plain and literal truth. Above all, he is more than just a herald of God's kingdom, more even than a regent of it under Yahweh. Contrary to expectation, he is more important than the kingdom itself, which exists for his sake and not the other way around. He is the inaugurator of the new and everlasting covenant foretold by Jeremiah, and the instrument of establishing it is his own blood shed in sacrifice. Finally, though he was truly put to death, he was just as truly restored to life, raised from the tomb by God's power; and he promises the same resurrection and similar glorious life to those who accept him as redeemer and put their faith in him.

Such might be a sketch of the high points of the Christian faith. My purpose has been to indicate the Old Testament foundation on which each of them rests. For the Christian, therefore, these ultimately make up the theological significance of the Old Testament.

**Index**

# Index